Enjoyment of the Same

A History of Public Lands in Southwest Florida

NICHOLAS G. PENNIMAN IV & FRANKLIN ADAMS

Barringer Publishing, Naples, Florida
www.barringerpublishing.com
Design and layout by Linda S. Duider

Cover photo by Clyde Butcher

ISBN 978-1-954396-35-7

Library of Congress Cataloging-in-Publication Data
Enjoyment of the Same:
A History of Public Lands in Southwest Florida

Printed in U.S.A.

CONTENTS

FOREWORD

This book began in an attempt to understand the origins and sources of a massive die off of Florida manatees in the Indian River Lagoon of Martin County on the east coast of Florida. There is a smaller, and genetically slightly different, population along the west coast, and the idea was to identify early steps to prevent a similar die off, particularly since the west coast had been hit hard by a 19-month red tide and blue-green algae outbreak in 2018 and 2019.

Working through the initial phase it soon became obvious that a great deal had already been written about the manatees and that state and federal wildlife managers were on top of it. In addition there were a number of nonprofit organizations intimately and directly involved. My focus for the past 20 years had been primarily on issues in southwest Florida and the Indian River lagoon was a long way away. It was time to shift gears.

While doing further research I had a conversation with Franklin Adams, who is a very large part of this book. We began to discuss how so much of Collier County—almost 70%—ended up as public lands and about how to make sure that future development was to the highest standards of land management. Adams had great experience with saving the Fakahatchee Strand and an ongoing love of the Turner River, a clear and free flowing stream that was part of his growing up in southwest Florida. As we talked about it, I realized that not only was the Turner its own story, but also a microcosm of the sweeping paradigm shift in the late 1960s to move away from unrestrained development and into an era of appreciation for, and the saving of, natural resources.

Franklin had saved a number of files from his environmental work over the years He was a close friend of Marjory Stoneman Douglas, author of *The Everglades: River of Grass*, and an outspoken advocate. His insights and recollections are all in his own words set out in italics in the text of this book. Some of the information contained in the documents has never been seen the light of day, and I realized that there was a story behind the conventional history that needed to be told that does not contradict but rather amplifies and illuminates how some of the choices were made during a time when vast expanses of land were considered for public purchase, offering an extraordinarily intimate look at how decisions were made at the highest levels in the State of Florida.

My appreciation goes to Ed Carlson, retired head of Audubon's Corkscrew Swamp Sanctuary for his time spent in conversation and to our cartographer John Beriault who endured Hurricane Ian and persevered through multiple revisions of his maps. To Jack Moller for providing the John Jones letters. Jeff Schlesinger of Barringer Publishing and I are now collaborating on our third book together. He is a delight to work with as is his staff in formatting and Linda Duider in enhancing the maps.

We are grateful to Clyde Butcher and his family for permission to use one of his creations as our cover and particularly appreciative of Paul Tilton, of the Clyde Butcher Gallery in Venice, for his assistance in getting the right image and best possible reproduction.

There are many books listed in the bibliography that tell stories in greater detail, and this book is intended to look at the history of public lands with less granularity. If you, as a reader, are interested in learning more search the bibliography; there are lot of good books there.

The title of this book, "Enjoyment of the Same," is taken directly from the opening sentence of the Organic Act of 1916 that created the National Park Service and empowered it to locate and manage national parks "... to conserve the scenery and the natural and historic objects and the wild life therein and and to provide for the enjoyment of the same...."

INTRODUCTION

The story of south Florida is a story of the water and the land, how they meet and how they interact to provide a rich subtropical but ever fragile landscape. The sheer productivity and resilience of nature provided thousands of years of resources to fulfill most all human needs. Then, development occurred with little thought as to the consequences and with much emphasis on man's right to take nature and mold it to fit immediate desires and rewards.

This book was inspired by the last paragraph of Ray Dasmann's great work published in 1967:

> "If you can't win the fight for Florida's environment, what can you win, and is it worth winning? Are you really prepared to acquiesce while the dredge-and-fill, the high-rise and the low-rise developments, the highways and the jet-ports, the barge canals and the industrial parks, cut the land to ribbons? Are you willing to wait until the pesticides accumulate and the wildlife has gone? While the waters of every stream and

lake and bay become choked and filthy? Will you be willing to steer your little boat down a dirty canal into a fishless ocean? Do you really want to make extra money at the expense of your home country, knowing it can buy you only a little more of what you already have in surfeit, knowing it can buy you no refuge? Where do you go when all the fair places have been ruined? Where do you go from Florida?" [1]

In the late 1960s, the threat of development to the natural world awakened Floridians to the need for environmental protection. The groundwork had been laid by Marjory Douglas' book *The Everglades: River of Grass* and by Rachel Carson's *Silent Spring.* But a few books, as alarming as they were, did little to spur action. It took a proposal to build the largest airport in the world, capable of handling supersonic passenger jets, right in the middle of south Florida. That began an era of restoring sensitive lands and water to their historic state. That process, seen in part through the eyes of a man who lived through that time and helped shape the changes that took place, is what this book is all about.

Franklin Adams, for some of his career, was a fishing guide and ecotour operator out of Everglades City. A native Floridian born in Miami, his father brought him to the Big Cypress as a present for his seventh birthday. He never forgot the wild landscape and moved to southwest Florida as a young man in the early 1950s, where he quickly grew to love the pristine wilderness. And as he saw it being compromised by roads and development, entered a second phase of his life as an official of the Izaak Walton League and Florida Wildlife Federation, both of which gave him platforms from which he could fight for the preservation and restoration of the world he so deeply cared for.

I was a friend of Marjory Douglas and part of the early Friends of the Everglades effort to have the Big Cypress named a National Preserve. Then, through some of my other activities became deeply involved in the formation of a number of large conservation project in particular the Turner River and the Fakahatchee Strand.

Throughout this book the reader will find quotations in italics and shadow-boxes. Those are either words from interviews, or direct quotes from letters and private notes written by Adams. They are intended to amplify and illuminate the issues and events being written about, but before digging into history it is helpful to briefly summarize the underlying premise that informs this book—all about two topics: the water and the land.

WATER: THE BASIS OF LIFE

Florida is all about water. The state averages 55 inches of rainfall every year. Sometimes more. Downpours in the summer recharge high level and deeper aquifers throughout the state. The surficial aquifers are used for homeowner's wells. In the dry season, November through April, those deeper aquifers are slowly drawn down to provide water to the urban areas along the coast.

Beneath all lies the Floridan aquifer, a massive underground river of fresh water, beginning in Georgia and Alabama and passing through the northern two thirds of the state near the surface. It is the source for the iconic springs like Homosassa and Weekiwatchee and Silver and a source of water for number of developments.

As the aquifer passes south below the middle of the state, it gradually dives lower. By the time it reaches the Everglades it is 1,000 feet below the surface. The main source of water inland comes from several shallow sand aquifers replenished by rainfall. In the coastal areas near Fort Myers and Naples, the Hawthorn aquifer and Tamiami formation, heavily layered with confining limestone, provide water to urban areas.

On the east coast, Broward, Miami-Dade, and parts of Monroe County are all served by the Biscayne aquifer, completely unrelated to the underground storage areas on the west coast, but inexorably tied to the Everglades.

LAND: SOUTH FLORIDA TO THE COAST

The geology of south Florida was formed by nearly infinite layers of microorganisms, mainly calcium-based, deposited over millions of years and compressed into thick layers beginning 550 thousand years ago. The Florida peninsula began to emerge about 35 million years ago and the limestone began to harden. The northern half of the state was never again underwater, but the south half was flooded until 25 million years ago. As the planet went through warming and cooling cycles, habitat and plant communities adapted to changing conditions until the Wisconsin glacial maximum about 25,000 years ago when climate had cooled and the glaciers reached their peak coverage in North America. At the time, the western shore of Florida was 250 km farther out.

As the climate warmed and glaciers retreated, the southern third of the Florida Peninsula became an extensive subtropical wetland. It included the Everglades, the singular path of sheet flow from Lake Okeechobee oozing down to today's Everglades National Park. A vast wilderness, the Everglades was characterized by a distant horizon after endless miles of saw grass, interrupted by an occasional cypress hammock. Teeming with wildlife like the giant sloth and mammoths, it was hooded by buzzards circling on the thermals rising from the sun-drenched moist ground. In the wet season towering cumulus clouds formed massive thunderheads and moved toward the west coast pushed along by the offshore wind. Much of that can still be seen today; and there is still only one Everglades in the world.

Coastal Estuaries Ecosytem

From the central Everglades to the southwest lies Everglades National Park. Dedicated in 1947, it has been subjected to sporadic moments of marginal abuse but has survived to become one of America's great parks. Directly to the west are a collection of parks, preserves, and wildlife protected areas. It's to those that we now turn, to take a high level look at what they are today, followed by a series of chapters of how each came into public ownership for the use and enjoyment of all.

OKEECHOBEE BASIN AND THE EVERGLADES

The Okeechobee basin is a very small area just south of the lake. Over the centuries decaying plants formed a layer of muck, ranging in depth from two to fifteen feet deep. The soil formed was highly productive and ended up as the northern part of what is now known as the Everglades Agricultural Area (EAA).

Immediately to the south are the greater central Everglades, a low-lying basin between the Southern Atlantic Coastal Strip on the east and Big Cypress Swamp to the west, characterized by a gradual descent from north to south with a gradient of approximately 13 feet from the Okeechobee basin to Everglades National Park. Water oozes nearly 100 miles from the Okeechobee basin, down to the park and out the Shark River Slough into Florida Bay, moving at approximately 1 km per day depending on rainfall amounts.

The Everglades hard bottom underlay is a porous carbonate rock—known as karst. Since carbonate formation is the result of accretion of natural materials like sand and shells, it is inherently soft and easy to penetrate. As plants die the detritus tends be highly acidic and dissolves the rock as it seeps through cracks and small pores. These fractures developed over many thousands of years and significantly altered the layer underlying the Everglades.

BIG CYPRESS

To the west is today's 728,000 acre Big Cypress. It is characterized as a swamp since it is forested by bands of cypress trees, separated by marshy areas which dry up in the winter. Cypress domes grow in bedrock depressions where the soft surface has collapsed and peat soil has accumulated with the deepest toward the center of the depression.

The preserve had little to offer humans apart from gigantic old growth trees, rising as high as 120 feet, much in demand for durability and water resistance. As a geologic sub-province it begins at the western edge of the central Everglades, is bounded just north of Interstate 75 and on the west by the Fakahatchee Strand Preserve State Park. Higher than the central Everglades and bordered by the Sha-Ha-Lege ledge, it ranges from 12 to 39 feet above sea level along the northern and eastern edge sloping to the south and west where it terminates only slightly above sea level in the mangrove forests of the coast. At the base of the swamp are layers of sand and silt and minerals, covering porous limestone through which water can be filtered and cleansed. Fed by seasonal inundation from rainfall, the fresh water ends up at the shoreline of the coastal fringe known as the Ten Thousand Islands.

The Big Cypress watershed is a monster. It feeds into a part of Everglades National Park, and is a vast hydrologic ecosystem that functionally interconnected these natural areas before roads and canals moved in. With the relatively low gradient, there are multiple plant communities within the preserve, mainly cypress domes and strands in the wetlands and hardwood forests at higher elevations along the edges of marshes. It manifests a primitive beauty, home to swamp ferns, myriad orchids, bromeliads and other epiphytes, all included in the over 800 species of vascular flora in the swamp. Riven by multiple strands and depressed flow ways, civilization is far removed; the solitude of the swamp embraces and engulfs the visitor.

Being in essence a large wetland, the Big Cypress has the capacity to remove nutrients and particulate matter on a constant and ongoing basis. Despite this, some of the water moving to the west and southwest is still impaired with nutrient pollution.

Because of canals and other constructed diverters, hydrologic unity in the Big Cypress does not exist today. Many of the named preserves that follow in this chapter including the Fakahatchee Strand Preserve State Park, Collier Seminole State Park and the Ten Thousand Islands, Rookery Bay National Estuarine Research Reserve, and the newly restored Picayune Strand State Forest are today all parts of a disconnected ecosystem. Plans to restore nature's flow are being made and remade almost every month, and those plans will be examined in detail in later chapters of this book.

FAKAHATCHEE STRAND

The Fakahatchee Strand Preserve State Park is a subtropical swamp approximately 20 miles long and 5 miles wide running from north to south. Its 85,000 acres are part of the hydrology of the Big Cypress system where fresh water drains south into the Ten Thousand Islands. It is a mixed swamp forest where bedrock is close to the surface with a protective over story of swamp trees and saturated soil capable of fostering the growth of highly sensitive tropical plants.

The Fakahatchee was logged heavily from 1944 to 1957 for its thousands of old growth cypress trees requiring construction of tram roads to provide access. By 1948 the south half of the strand had been depleted with as much as 1 million board feet taken out every week.

Flanked on the east by the Big Cypress and the Barron River canal the strand is fed water from the large sloughs to the north—both of which have been declared impaired. The underlying geology of the strand is very similar to that of the Everglades and rest of the Big Cypress. But most importantly, the Fakahatchee is the largest wetland receptor of water from the Okaloacoochee Slough making it the major drainage conduit into the estuaries of the coast.

The Fakahatchee is bounded on the west by the newly restored Picayune Strand State Forest. To the north the Camp Keais Slough and Corkscrew Swamp today have a tenuous hydrologic connection to the strand, but prior to development of Fort Myers and Naples, and uninterrupted by developments roads and canals, water flow was continuous.

In addition to a variety of wildlife the strand has the largest concentration and diversity of native orchids in North America—most famous for being home of the ghost orchid, subject of Susan Orleans book *"The Orchid Thief"* and a later movie. But the ghost is only one of 95 plant species in the Fakahatchee considered as endangered, threatened or of special concern. The royal palms in the strand are the most extensive in the world. And, it is home to 12 species of plants that cannot be found anywhere else in North America.

PICAYUNE STRAND

To the west of the Fakahatchee is another important subset of the Big Cypress basin flow system—the Picayune Strand State Forest. It is now the fourth largest state forest in Florida comprised of 78,000 acres bordered by Alligator Alley on the north and incorporating South Belle Meade to the west. It consists primarily of cypress swamps and wet prairie areas as well as pine flatwoods located in southernmost section. A hydric forest, it is typical of an area with nearly level sandy soil and slow drainage so is under water from May to November when its wetlands historically perform two important functions: first they contribute heavily to groundwater recharge and second, ease the flow of water into the estuaries to the south, discharging directly into the Ten Thousand Islands and Rookery Bay.

Like the Fakahatchee, a small part of the Picayune was logged in the 1940s and 1950s. After being depleted it was purchased by the developers of Cape Coral, the Rosen brothers from Baltimore who built twenty foot wide roads crisscrossing the landscape and canals draining the wetlands, creating an alien habitat welcoming to non-native vegetation.

In the 1970s it became obvious that the canals were destroying the downstream ecosystems. In 1985 the State of Florida, using the 1979 Conservation and Recreation Lands Act began to purchase the land from approximately 17,000 owners in what was once called Southern Golden Gate Estates. Some parts of the project, notably the Faka Union Canal and a small development with a marina called Port of the Islands would have to remain. They are there today. The canal outlet created a point source of discharge upsetting the balance of fresh and saltwater in the Ten Thousand Islands—resulting in a significant loss of wildlife and a severe decrease in nature's immobile vacuum cleaners—sea grasses and oyster beds.

ROOKERY BAY & TEN THOUSAND ISLANDS

The Ten Thousand Islands extends for 60 miles along the edge of Florida's southern Gulf Coast from Cape Romano (at the south end of Marco Island) to the outlet of the Shark River in Everglades National Park. The coastal terrain and feed-in rivers were formed by a series of sea level fluctuations as glacial ice moved in and out of the shoreline. While the ice never reached as far as the Ten Thousand Islands, massive amounts of sediment were pushed onto the peninsula, combining with the detritus of aquatic life to create a carbonate substrate. That bedrock slope decreases moving south. In the Ten Thousand Islands, it is estimated at 0.34 m/km whereas by the Shark River it is down to 0.12 m/km.[2]

There are currently two separately managed parts to the Ten Thousand Islands. First is the 27,000 acre Cape Romano—Ten Thousand Islands Aquatic Preserve. Established in October 1969 it was one of the first aquatic preserves in Florida created by a program designed to protect estuaries in a fully natural condition. The northern part is managed by the Rookery Bay National Estuarine Research Reserve which also has jurisdiction over the Rookery Bay Aquatic Preserve just to the north. The southern part of the Ten Thousand Islands protected area begins south of Everglades City and runs along the coastal fringe of Everglades National Park. The park manages that segment.

In addition to melting ice and rising sea level, the humble oyster was critical to the formation of the coastal ecosystem. Immobile as adults they feed on whatever food passes by. The faster the current moves the happier they are. They grow best in tidal areas near rivers and outlets where salinity is lower than the Gulf which averages about 36 parts per thousand and where hard bottom needs to be available for the oysters to tie into; a sediment bottom is useless.

In tidal areas, where the water moves back and forth, oysters tend to orient themselves cross-tide. In other words, they will take an east-west position if the tides are moving north-south allowing tides to bring phytoplankton and small algae into their filtration system. By situating themselves perpendicular to the tidal flow, they increase the velocity of tidal changes around the congregations and start to catch soil and sediment as it is carried down the rivers from inland.

They also block red mangrove propagules as they emerge from the coastal forests. The propagules (seeds) look like a small pencils floating vertically. Mangroves maintain their propagules until germinated. Once they fall into the water from the parent tree they float horizontally but eventually swell up. The heavy end sinks so that when the propagule finally washes up against an oyster bar or shoal with sufficient sediment it quickly takes root and sprouts leaves. The process takes only a few months. Driven by wind and gulf currents along the coast they become trapped by oyster beds to grow in the rich soup and eventually become islands.

In a way oyster-beds that created mangrove islands cause self-inflicted destruction of the colonies. As tree cover on the islands spreads and expands, the flow channels feeding nutrients to the oysters becomes restricted. As a result, the oysters die off leaving their limestone shells as a memorial to their work in forming yet another mangrove sanctuary for the small fish, crabs and other creatures seeking protection from predators.

REDUX

To recap, the Big Cypress and Ten Thousand Islands combine to form a highly productive ecosystem. Freshwater from rainfall generates 98% of the water in the Big Cypress.

The balance comes from a few springs at the headwaters of rivers that flow gradually toward the coast and mix with the salt water of the Gulf. In those estuaries, the extensive root system of the red mangrove forms a protective nursery for 80% of the fish species found in South Florida. While the central Everglades suffered devastating damage from ditches, dams, canals and levees obstructing and diverting the slow-moving sheet flow of water southward from Lake Okeechobee to Florida Bay, the Big Cypress and Ten

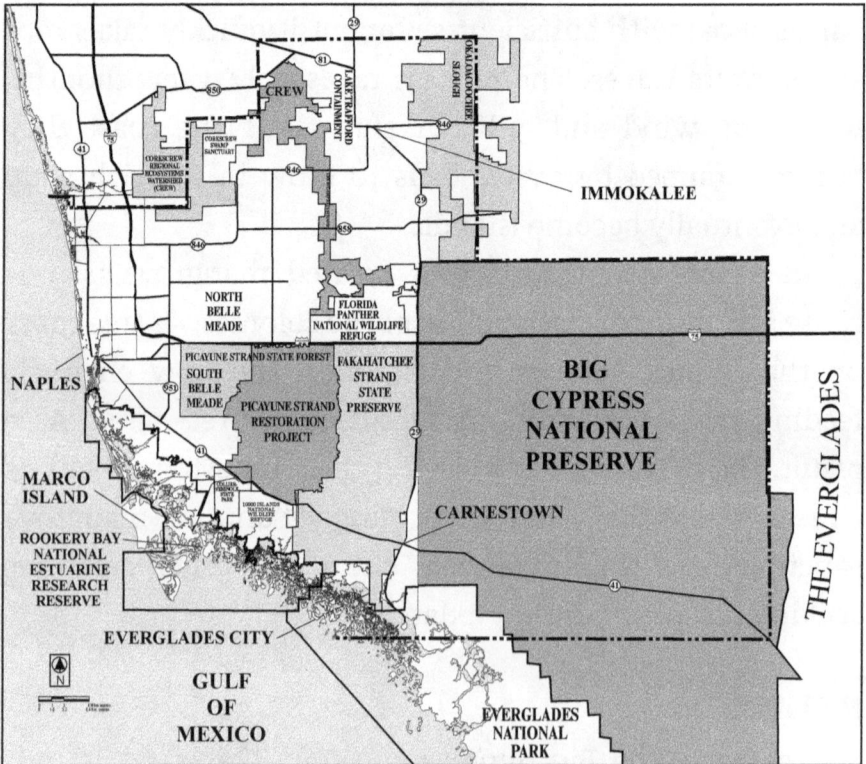

Collier County noting all public lands.
Dotted dashed line is the Collier County border.
Map created by John G. Beriault.

Thousand Islands have not suffered the same degree of impairment.

The places described above were historically interconnected forming a unitary ecosystem, but no longer. There are now warning signs visible to all. Dying sea grasses, increasing frequency and severity of red tide outbreaks, increasing turbidity of rivers coming out of the Big Cypress, and the gradual reduction in bivalve mollusks and fish populations, are all the result of continuous pressure from development in the rural lands of Collier County. It is overwhelming natural systems and gradually polluting the coast as described in the words of Franklin Adams:

The Big Cypress Swamp and the Ten Thousand Islands have been adversely impacted by the same causes that damaged the Glades. Fresh water in the proper seasonal amounts no longer flows through the Big Cypress Swamp into the estuaries of the Ten Thousand Islands. All of south Florida is stressed, the fishing, both commercial and sport, continues to decline in spite of bag limits, closures and size limits. It's the water, in the proper season of the year, in proper amounts and of good quality. The Everglades was once a great and resilient system. We have brought it to its knees in a manner of speaking. It's up to us to push for its restoration.

All the places named above would eventually come into public ownership. That story will be told in later chapters, but now we turn to the origins of the human presence in south Florida beginning when ice covered vast areas of the northern hemisphere, dropping the level of the Gulf of Mexico as much as 100 meters, exposing the Florida platform reaching out 250 km to the west when humans crossed the Siberian land bridge and moved quickly south.

Coming of People

FLORIDA'S EARLY HUMANS

For thousands of years, south Florida was a swamp populated with savage beasts surviving in a kill or be killed world, violent, brutal and uncaring as to what species survived as experimentation led to adaptation. Infested with swarms of mosquitoes and subject to periodic storm-induced inundation it was inhospitable to human occupation. It was an ecosystem in perfect balance.

Humans eventually came. Known as Paleoindians, they migrated from Asia by foot and by boat beginning 12,000 years ago when the Laurentide glacier had sucked up enough sea water to expose a land bridge across the Bering Sea. Canada was a mass of ice, with either a few corridors to pass through, or the coastline to pass around. Moving quickly south toward warmer weather, the new arrivals found a pleasant climate in Florida with a land mass nearly double what it is today where large animals such as mammoth and bison roamed in abundance and Gulf coast waters provided marine life for food year-round. Life was good, but they faced one problem: a reliable source of fresh water.

As archeologists sifted through evidence of human occupation, they concluded that water then, as today, was the primary factor in deciding where to locate settlement sites. There were few rivers. The most abundant inland sources lay in the northern two-thirds of state where it was elevated, sitting on the Pamlico Terrace near modern Ocala, as much as 25 feet higher than the southern third. (This is obvious when driving north of Lake Okeechobee.)

The earliest human occupation in south Florida was probably an area called Little Salt Spring near Sarasota used as a hunting site around 10,000 years ago. Since animals congregated at watering holes, it was a preferred kill site for large fauna and a number of fossil bones have been found at the bottom of the sinkhole. In addition, the slough draining out of the pond was filled with mortuary burials ranging from 6,800 to 5,200 years ago.[3]

In southwest Florida at that time the water table was close to 100 meters lower than at present.[4] Since fresh water was hard to find people stayed in the north and central part of the state for the next 4,000 years where there were multiple springs from the Floridan aquifer lying close to the surface. Lake Okeechobee had not yet come into existence.

At the glacial peak time, the southwest coastline was as much as 250 kilometers west of its present location and as the glaciers melted, the Gulf rose, forcing indigenous people to move gradually inland changing their campsites and villages with some frequency, leaving any archaeological evidence under the rising waters of the Gulf.

As the millennia passed, the climate stabilized. Survival and eventually comfort was becoming less a matter of adapting to changing environmental conditions and more a matter of manipulating the natural world. Rivers were forming throughout north Florida and rainfall was abundant in the south during the wet season as the runoff remained fresh up to the salt line—however there was still little fresh water available. The level of the Gulf rose more gradually after about 3,500 before the current era (BCE) and the inland water table of the Big Cypress began to stabilize, allowing fresh water to settle in ponds and wetlands.

Fresh water pockets began to form, probably as rainfall was sequestered in slight depressions. A few deeper artesian wells were on present-day Marco Island and Chokoloskee, but there were also small surficial aquifers on Cape Romano, Lostman's Key, Gomez Key and Sand Key. All of these were known and available to the people living along the coast with their maritime adaptation. In addition there were fresh water "lenses" out in the Gulf near Cape Romano and offshore near Naples and in channels in the Ten Thousand Islands, but it is unlikely that the shore-adapted tribes either knew about or exploited them.

As the population increased, social complexity developed, and permanent settlements began to form with large coastal shell mounds, created from the detritus of millions of meals from the abundant oysters and clams, where the sea breeze blew away clouds of mosquitoes and minimized inundation during tropical downpours.

GLADES PEOPLE

Much of archeological evidence depends upon pottery, which with carbon dating provides the current temporal model for human occupation of Southwest Florida. There is still some controversy about dates, but not about environmental alterations. They were relatively minor and short-lived.

The Glades people began to settle in the Ten Thousand Islands around 5,500 years ago as sea level rise slowed. One very early site on Horr's Island (near today's Marco Island) has four fairly large mounds and one shell ring with one of the mounds carbon-dated to approximately 6,700 years ago. The overall elevation of Horr's Island, from 3 to 15 meters above mean sea level, made it ideal for permanent settlement during the Paleoindian period. Despite fluctuations in the glacier melt and resulting sea level rise, the island stayed dry.

Popular history promotes the presence of the Calusa throughout southwest Florida at this time but the pottery was relatively simple and undecorated so the evidence indicates that people populating the coast south of Charlotte Harbor were probably separate, and not necessarily subservient, to the later powerful, militaristic and hegemonous Calusa. With adequate resources there would be no reason to pay tribute to a dominant hierarchy. Stratified societies, before European contact, tended to occur in locations where crops such as corn could be grown and stored to be distributed as necessary during times of scarcity. In coastal areas such as the Pacific Northwest and south Florida, where there were adequate food sources, indigenous societies tended to be less stratified and based upon smaller units such as families and cooperative groups.

While the exploitation of some coastal resources required cooperation, there is little evidence, other than Horr's Island, of permanent settlements. Small groups probably moved from the coast to temporary inland hunting camps on a nomadic basis.

By around 750 current era (CE), pottery in the Glades culture area began to show more decoration and incising. This alteration indicated trade and an exchange of ideas and design among tribal groups. By 900 CE art forms had shifted from animalistic to anthropomorphic, a sign that the more militant and ritual-oriented Calusa to the north had begun to assimilate the relatively benign Glades culture to the south.

The Calusa were highly organized. They built canals, such as the one bisecting Pine Island, to allow dugouts to transport people and goods along a direct route rather than having to use nature's winding, and ever-changing, waterways of south Florida's coast. Nature provided the raw materials for tools and personal adornment. Large whelks, with the outer shell penetrated by a wooden haft, became an effective mallet-type tool for pounding. Shark's teeth and scallop shells were ideally suited to necklaces for personal decoration. The lowly and common palmetto frond was a tough, fibrous material readily available to be woven into baskets and fishing nets.

The timing and extent of Calusa control is hard to establish, but throughout southwest Florida it is clear that larger groups became the norm, and that ritual, a key element in Calusa culture, was clearly in play uncovered by archeological finds such as Frank Hamilton Cushing's excavation famous for its feline statuette carved from native wood known as the Key Marco Cat.

TURNER RIVER SITE

Upstream from the mouth of the Turner River is a large archaeological site. It covers 30 acres and is populated by 30 shell mounds. Archaeological excavation in 1955 estimated occupation from as early as 200 BCE to 900 CE which places it in the early Calusa period.

The Turner River historically was a slow moving stream about 9 miles long emptying into present-day Everglades National Park at Chokoloskee. It moved through hardwood forests and wet prairies as the elevation declined until reaching the mangrove estuary of the coast. By providing a source of fresh water, the river created an ideal environment for sea grasses which tolerate salinity of between 20 to 35 parts per thousand (ppt). It was a favorite spot for the Florida manatee as well, with both factors accounting for its value as a large village site.

One conclusion emerged from the temporal sequence of the mounds: people were moving toward, not away, from the water. Since the river was the primary source for food, this made sense.[5] The mounds extended outward into the flow of the tidal river; based upon their proximity to one another it is possible the gaps were used as opening to fish traps.[6]

FISH TRAPS

An entirely different type of construction existed at the outflow bay of Henderson Creek in Rookery Bay. Shell Island Road ends at the remains of a once large shell mound covering about one acre to a height of 30' It was excavated to build the roadbed to Marco Island, but is a reminder that there was once a large nucleated settlement. Across the bay in a tidal setting, is a series of interconnected shell middens (but not mounds) that form the walls of large entrapments that might have been used to keep fish fresh and available.[7] Using weighted palmetto frond nets and dugout canoes, certain species could be herded into the constructed impoundments. Once in, a net drawn across the mouth of the storage bay would prevent the prey from escaping nature's refrigerator, where fish and dolphins and manatees could be preserved until easily harvested.

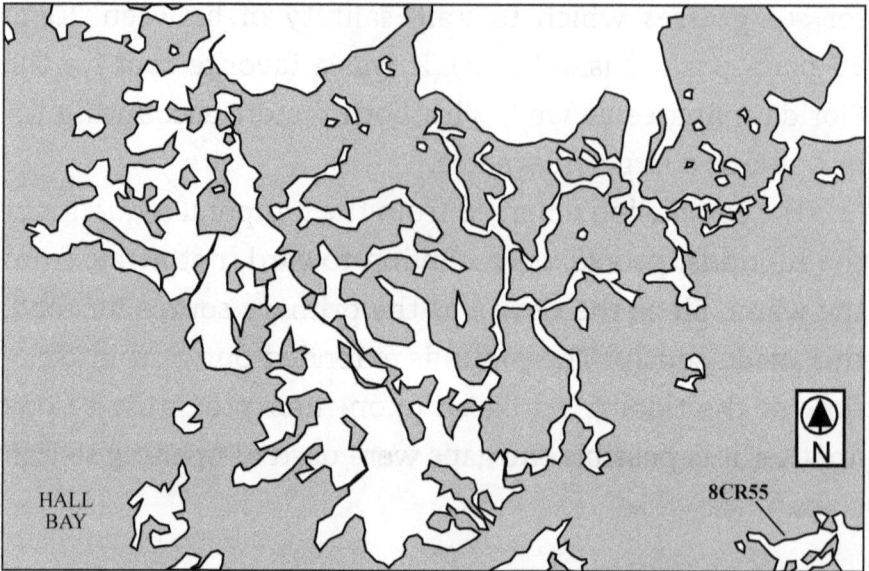

Henderson Creek outlet across from 8CR55.[8]
Map created by John G. Beriault.

_____

If in fact the area shown, based upon aerial photographs, is for storing of fish and large mammals, it provides the basis for several hypotheses about early human occupation in the Ten Thousand Islands. First, management of net fishing required both cooperation and direction. Many forms of human activity involve expertise or leadership for specific tasks. In fishing, some individuals are simply better at it than others, and those who have the ability to achieve desired outcomes by organizing people into a cooperative endeavor are generally favored. This doesn't necessarily lead to the conclusion that coordinating and organizing efforts translated into political or tribal power, but was simply a function of the need to exploit resources in the most efficient manner.

Second, there were only a few spots along the coast where palmetto, the most common cordage used in weaving nets, grew. Other sources such as yucca had to be found nearby or palmetto fiber had to be imported, an indication of trade and/or inter-local cooperation.

Third, the capture and entrapment of large mammals would be based upon optimal foraging strategy. This theory, in its simplest form, states that the most calories gained for the fewest calories expended is the basis of human choices as to what to hunt. In tidal areas the most desirable would be dolphins or a large mammal, like the passive manatee that could be easily herded into storage bays, and provide weeks of nourishment.

Lastly, not all fishing grounds were equal. Control of this resource may have been a matter of either who got there first or could indicate ownership based upon lineage or power. The most productive fishing grounds would have been utilized first, and as family and tribal groups moved in later they would tend to occupy areas less productive or more difficult to manage.

The location of villages also depended upon the availability of fresh water. With only a few springs in the coastal zone of Southwest Florida below the Caloosahatchee River, fresh and potable water had to be captured either in cisterns during the wet season which required constant attention and management, or from freshwater lenses in the limestone substrate, or in rivers and ponds. Agricultural villages would necessarily be located where the soil was rich and fresh water could be captured and stored for irrigation.

Minor environmental manipulation in south Florida prior to European contact was designed to facilitate food production and trade. The remnants of an early human presence have faded, the canals filled in, and shell mounds excavated as the base for roads. While land-based megafauna became extinct, aquatic food sources like manatees and dolphins were able to regenerate over time. Rich soil, created by plant decay, washed out of inland sources, and formed fertile areas for farming. Estuaries were unharmed by excess nutrients, fresh water was available but limited, and the stage was set for the next influx of humans, those bent upon conquest and seeking treasure.

SPANISH

Florida migrants from Asia, after occupying the coast and inland hunting camps for nearly 7,000 years, began to encounter white men in unofficial trading expeditions from Cuba in the early 16th century on both the east and west coast with some regularity.

The Portuguese had visited Florida in 1502 looking for slaves to work sugar plantations in the Caribbean and Brazil, but were unsuccessful and abandoned the effort due to increasing harassment by the more powerful Spanish navy.

As tales of a powerful, militant group filtered back to Cuba, the king decided to send an emissary to assay the situation. Ponce de Leon visited the Calusa capital, probably at Mound Key in Charlotte Harbor, in 1513. According to Spanish records, the island had a large internal canal to welcome visitors. Flanked on both sides by tall and decorated Calusa warriors the entry was designed to intimidate.

In my first year at Miami High School. I discovered a book in the card catalog under "Everglades." It was Marjory Stoneman Douglas' "River of Grass." I checked it out, read it, and was captivated by its message. So I read it a second time. Later, when attending Miami Dade Junior College South as it was then called, I saw that Marjory Douglas would be a visiting lecturer on "The Natural History of South Florida." I immediately signed up.

I can truly say I never enjoyed a course or lecture series as much as I did that semester listening to Marjory. When she described the Spanish landing on the coast of Florida her rich flowing descriptions painted what I would call word pictures. You could hear the wind in the galleon's rigging, the creak and groans of the ship's timbers and the straining of the anchor rode as it rose and fell on the ocean swells. You could almost smell the dampness of the ships' holds and see the Indians peering from the interior at something they had never seen before.

The Spanish were looking for gold, having found treasure in South and Central America, but found none in the Calusa Empire. Following initial contact, relationships between the tribe and the Spanish were never comfortable, and in one encounter de Leon was struck by an arrow. He left Florida and went to Cuba where he died of his wound. Despite finding no trove of treasure the Catholic Church, tied closely to the Spanish crown, began to proselytize. A few attempts by Franciscans to start missions in south Florida met with mixed results, and the Spanish found that settling in northern Florida involved less conflict than trying to coexist with the militants on the southwest coast.

The Spanish incursion, unsuccessful by their pecuniary standards, had a dire consequence. Local populations, with no immunity against diphtheria, measles, typhoid and smallpox, were decimated. Estimates of losses across the entire state amounted to as much as 80%, but the geographically dispersed coastal adaptation probably reduced the incidence of mortality.[9]

SEMINOLE OCCUPATION

After the Spanish war the British took control of Florida from 1763 to 1783. They concentrated efforts in the northeast part of the state and up into the Carolinas using slaves from the Caribbean for work in the cotton fields and rice plantations—one leg of the infamous Triangle. In south Florida, ravaged by disease and with a population of less than 100 souls, the last of the Calusa departed for Cuba or the Florida Keys.[10]

The British deeded Florida back to Spain in 1783, but by that time the United States had won the War of Independence. The Spanish presence was only nominal and barely noticed as the United States moved to consolidate territory and began to assert control of the region west of Florida with an enhanced military after the Louisiana Purchase of 1803.

In the meantime, the indigenous population of Florida was undergoing a gradual change. After the Calusa emigrated, the state was occupied over time by tribes from north of Florida. Escaping the slave colonies of Georgia and South Carolina, members of the loose-knit Creek Confederacy, including the Oconee, moved south. Primarily agriculturalists, and settling in arable areas suitable for farming and cattle, they were augmented in the early 19th century by a large contingent of Red Stick Creeks when, defeated by Andrew Jackson at Horseshoe Bend in 1814, they retreated into north Florida.[11]

Jackson, intent on eliminating all Native Americans from the face of the earth, and ignoring the political niceties of treaties and Spanish ownership, moved south in 1817 to press his case against natives with the First Seminole

War. His incursion forced the Spanish to confront military reality and in 1819 the United States negotiated a deal to purchase Florida. By 1821 under terms of the Adams-Onis Treaty, the United States took full possession and military control of Florida. The Indian killer, Andrew Jackson, was appointed commissioner of the territory.

Most of the campaigns during the First Seminole War were conducted in the northern part of the state where a number of escaped slaves were hiding and by 1823 an attempt was made to settle the Indians in a reservation just north of Lake Okeechobee regardless of tribal allegiances. The effort was only marginally successful and a few Indians moved out of the reservation finding rich, fertile soil and fresh water along the Peace and Caloosahatchee rivers.

There was little interest in proceeding with further removal until 1837 when the United States Army built a fort on Rattlesnake Hammock, just east of present day Naples, across an old Indian pathway at the headwaters of Henderson Creek. In order to probe south and east the Army then built Fort Cass at the edge of the Okaloacoochee Slough and another where the Caloosahatchee River originates at Lake Okeechobee.

Small battles were fought over the next few years. The Seminoles, led by a military genius named Osceola, used hit and run techniques successfully developed in the American Revolution. However, his success was short-lived as he died of a throat infection in 1838.

Osceola's troops, despite his death, refused to surrender. The military then started a campaign in 1841 pushing down the coast past the present-day Turner River and reaching as far south as the Chatham River. It was the first extensive attempt by the Army to probe the coastal waters south of Marco Island. There were a few farms tended by small groups of natives with livestock, mainly oxen. The Army spent its energy burning dwellings and killing animals to deprive the Indians of food, but the results were deemed not worth the effort and the war wound down with no real conclusion.

Florida was granted statehood in March 1845. The Second Seminole War was over but the fertility of land directly south of Lake Okeechobee had been noted by Army officers and President James Polk, a strong believer in manifest destiny, decided to investigate. Selected for the job was Buckingham Smith, a St. Augustine lawyer and political figure prone to flowery prose and lengthy memoranda. After visiting the area he wrote in his report that the muck south of Lake Okeechobee "... is highly suited to the cultivation of sugar, rice, tobacco, cotton or corn." [12]

Then, in 1849 the Congress began to debate the Swamp Land Act, which would deed title of federal wetlands to the states in return for a promise to drain and convert the land to agricultural use. The act passed in 1850 and Florida was awarded 81,000 sq. km—mainly the Everglades. [13]

Hopeful that this would create a financial windfall, Florida decided to press yet again for Indian removal since the swamp land awarded was exactly where they lived. After a lengthy negotiation the government's agent at the time, Luther Blake, made one final monetary offer to the Seminoles. Instantly rejected, in response Florida attempted to raise $2 million to fund a militia, but with money hard to come by, asked Washington to increase pressure on the Indians and the War Department began to reactivate forts from the Second Seminole War—Fort Myers being one.

Federal patrols began to probe and burn Seminole camps, particularly the one at Deep Lake, a place where fresh water was readily available and the Indians had crops and citrus. After a series of Army raids Chief Billy Bowlegs had enough and ambushed a small patrol. With that provocation, the Third Seminole War began. Lasting for three years, it was marked by raids, ambushes and small engagements, but no decisive pitched battles. It became a war of attrition. The Indians were being pushed southward. Spread throughout the Big Cypress, they had their small settlements attacked, fields destroyed and houses burned until Bowlegs negotiated a monetary settlement, the Treaty of Moultrie Creek, part of which was an agreement that the Indians would depart South Florida in 1858 and move west to a reservation set aside in Oklahoma. Most of the Seminoles departed on steamers for New Orleans and made their way west, but not all. Those who remained found ways to thrive by engaging in trade for crops and animal skins.

Chief Osceola's troops were never conquered, but after nearly 50 years of sporadic military engagements the Seminole Wars made occupation of large nucleated villages few and far between as the Indians had been forced into continually moving into temporary campsites until found by the Army and forced to move again. As such those encampments did nothing to modify the balance of nature in existing ecosystems. What it did was eventually compress the Seminole population into inland areas leaving the coast available and open for White settlers to come. Then, the country was ripped apart by a war between the states.

THE SEMINOLE TRADE

The remnants of the Seminole tribe remaining in south Florida, around two hundred in number, were relatively undisturbed by the Civil War. Having known and worked the land for generations they were good farmers and good hunters. According to one source, living in clan camps they began to farm upland areas and tree hammocks in the Big Cypress, growing rice, corn, tobacco, potatoes and sugar cane—mainly for sustenance—and to raise cattle.[14] Upland areas of the Big Cypress Swamp were ideal for grazing. With a lack of fencing and open range, cattle mingling early White settlers and Seminoles was inevitable, but there was a willingness to work together in separating out ownership. And with increasing cooperation came trade, lasting for about 40 years from 1870 to 1910. The Indians would either barter or sell some vegetables. For substantial trade goods, they hunted deer and otter for pelts, but there is little record of the full extent of their commercial activities and it seemed to be a matter of "live and let live" in preference to open hostility.

Many White settlers were also hunters and by 1879 complaints were being registered by the Indians as some of the species were getting scarce. But one trade good that remained highly available was the alligator.[15] The Seminoles were generally settled inland and as the price of the reptile's hides for purses, belts and shoes rose they found a good way to make money. Alligators can survive temporarily in salt water, but prefer fresh lacking the salt glands of the crocodile. They congregate in isolated wetlands during the dry season, so were easy to find. It is estimated that between 1880 and 1894 Florida hunters, both native and White, killed at least 2.5 million alligators.[16] As the land was beginning to be drained, changes to the underlying ecosystem began to destroy contiguous habitat for several animals hunted by the Indians.

The Seminole trade was little more than an exercise in toleration. The tribes were, in many ways, invisible to the growing presence of White farmers and settlers. Reconstruction and the advent of the Gilded Age brought about early attempts to drain the central Everglades and connect both east and west coast. To do so the State of

Florida simply appropriated land owned by the Indians. In a reprise of the rampant violation of treaties in the western states in the name of manifest destiny, Florida officials in the name of economic development paid little or no regard to any promises, even in writing, made to the native tribes.

Early Settlers

NOMADS, FARMERS AND TRADERS

South Florida was virtually unaffected by the Civil War. With the exception of a few battles in the northern half of the state, military operations were minimal. However, the remoteness of the Everglades and Ten Thousand Islands beckoned deserters from both sides of the conflict. As fugitives they wanted little known about them or their history, so there is no record other than an occasional mention of the elusive inhabitants—mainly drifters and grifters.

As Reconstruction plodded its messy path through the south in the three decades leading up to the turn of the century, there were other newcomers who sought fame and fortune. Some were builders and other hunters, some were planters and others loggers, but in every case it was the untouched natural resources of good land, big trees, and abundant wildlife that brought them to Florida.

The men and women who came were highly independent capable of living in a hostile environment. The sheer difficulty of navigating coastal mangrove forests drew people who simply wished to trade civilization for isolation sometimes as a matter of choice and other times as a matter of necessity. There was never a thought of finding ways to bring others in.

Silt along the rivers was rich in nitrogen and given the productivity of the soil, several small farms were started along the southwest coast. One of the first was along the shores of the Turner River eponymously named for Capt. Dick Turner who settled sometime around 1874. Another early pioneer was John Weeks, who had moved up and down the coast in the late 1870s looking for an appropriate place to locate his family. He laid claim to Chokoloskee Island, 150 acres as high as 20 feet above mean sea level, protected by a mangrove fringe. It was, and is, one of the highest points on the coast next only to Caxambas on Marco Island, and had two underground sources of water from artesian wells, a rarity in southwest Florida.

But Weeks' family did not like living apart from civilization and he soon granted a 50% interest in the island to Adolphus Santini from Sanibel Island then sold his remaining half to William von Pfister, a member of the Union Army who never lived there and later sold his interest to the Santini family who occupied the island from about 1880 to 1900.[17]

Everglade, now known as Everglades City, was first settled by William Allen Smith in about 1871. He gave his middle name to the river and owned the town site from 1873 to 1889 after which he returned to his original home in Key West and soon passed away. The Allen River ran along the west side of what is now a large town protected by a few small mangrove islands in the Marjory Stoneman Douglas Wilderness. The buying and selling slowed down around the turn of the century as a number of other families moved onto Chokoloskee to settle permanently. One of the most important was Ted Smallwood, who settled in 1897 and opened a small store. He bought out the Santini family in 1900 and eventually became a large landowner along with George Storter, another store owner already in business based a little further north at Everglade.

The Storter family grew cucumbers, tomatoes and eggplants. They first plowed ground in 1882, and sold their crops in Key West for transport north to urban markets. In 1883 Storter built a house, and in 1887 his son came with his family and for $800 purchased Allen's holdings which covered the entire town site.[18] George Storter, Jr. established a store in 1892 to accommodate both the robust Indian trade and a growing number of fishermen who came for the large tarpon out in the Gulf of Mexico. He also cut buttonwood for sale as stove wood.[19]

The stores owned by Smallwood and Storter played an important role in the burgeoning trade between the Indians and Whites. Much of the commercial activity during the time was based on growing vegetables and other products and transporting them to Key West. As noted earlier, the Seminoles who remained in their native habitat had hunting skills to produce hides, but in addition to alligators there was another nearly unlimited resource: millions of birds with gorgeous feathers.

The new settlers had advantages that the Seminoles never did—one being large steam-powered, and later gasoline powered, vessels that could take trade goods back and forth to Key West, a thriving center of economic activity that had grown from 2,000 souls in 1852 to near 10,000 by 1880 and was a major port for produce and vegetables being shipped to New York by boat. Farmers found they could grow almost anything in the lush subtropical environment of the Ten Thousand Islands including sugarcane, bananas, pineapples, and cabbages. With a few added nutrients the land was highly productive, and the farms were sustainable in the long term, despite the occasional hurricane.

Certain crops were found to grow better in different environments. For example, tomatoes were best grown on shell mounds. In heavier muck soil, even with sand content, sugarcane was the most profitable crop and could be either converted to syrup or sold as chewing stalks.

The coast was never able to support large citrus operations. There was less arable land than in the uplands of central Florida but a number of smaller groves were planted with moderate success and with a freeze destroying the citrus in central Florida in 1886, and another in 1894-1895 chilling agriculture in north Florida, Adolphus Santini experimented with a variety of fruit trees on Chokoloskee Island growing apples, oranges, guavas and bananas, while at the same time Ted Smallwood grew "pears," the local name for avocados, which he sold at the very fancy price of five cents each in Fort Myers.

PLUME HUNTERS

There was, however, one group of men after the Civil War who caused the near extinction of a number of bird species—and that was the plume hunters. Beginning around 1870 women fancied large hats decorated with feathers, and even stuffed birds, a trend that may have begun with Marie Antoinette. A desire for plumed hats spread quickly throughout the western world. The millinery industry appetite was insatiable, preferring feathers taken during mating season when they were most colorful.

The mangrove forests from Naples south were ideal nesting sites for egrets, heron, flamingos and roseate spoonbills and by 1886 over five million birds had been killed in Florida, amounting to 95% of the extant shore birds in the state.[20] One of the largest rookeries ever found in North America was at the Shark River on the southwest coast with a population of 1 million birds located on little mangrove islands and along the shore. The rookery was completely shot out by the mid-1890s.[21] Wholesale slaughter was made possible with modern shotguns with pellets capable of spreading out over a wide target area. The mating birds were plucked, carcasses discarded, and their offspring left to die.

As plume hats became the rage in New York, the Indians were able to guide hunters in and out of prized roost and nesting locations. Indigenous people also traded in bird plumes, but not to the extent that the White hunters and poachers did, mainly because they did not possess modern weapons, and they regarded birds as food, not as a source for decoration as did the Plains Indians.

In 1900 the federal government prohibited interstate commerce in feathers. It made little difference. As the slaughter continued, bills protecting birds were passed by the Florida legislature in 1901, and in 1903 President Theodore Roosevelt, appalled by the destruction, designated Pelican Island near Vero Beach as a wildlife refuge. Over time other areas were set aside as sanctuaries, but had little impact until enforcement began in earnest with heavy fines and possible jail time for offenders. As a result, the price rose due to diminished supply, and by 1915 it was $32 per oz.—identical to the price of gold.

Fortunately for the few remaining birds, World War I disrupted the trans-Atlantic trade and the plume fashion fad passed, but the damage had been done. South Florida's environment suffered severe damage—all because of human fascination with a feathered hat. But nature has a way of rejuvenating itself, and the wading bird population of south Florida eventually recovered—albeit only partially.

DRAINING THE 'GLADES

Early farmers along the southwest coast adapted their agricultural practices to the environment, and not the other way around, until 1881 when a Philadelphia contractor purchased 4 million acres from the State of Florida in the Kissimmee River basin north of Lake Okeechobee and began to dredge canals in order to covert the land to agriculture and create a waterway corridor to move crops from inland to the two coasts. Hamilton Disston never fulfilled his promise. That would happen later, so prior to World War I, coastal agriculture remained small farms utilizing existing resources as productively as possible with little environmental manipulation.

But the Disston misadventure had an important consequence: it opened the eyes of a number of entrepreneurs and capitalists to opportunities in Florida. In the early 1880s Henry Flagler began to run his railroad down the east coast while Henry Bradley Plant was laying tracks down to Tampa on the west coast. Plant had planned to run a line from there across the Everglades to meet up with Flagler but thought better of it after looking at the problems in laying roadbed and tracks through mucky wilderness. Since transportation at the time was mainly by boat along coastal routes, rail service would give burgeoning industries access to ports and new markets, and offer timber companies transport for logging the pine forests of north Florida and the tall trees in the Big Cypress.

Ever since the White man first came to Florida, most of them have viewed Florida, and particularly the Everglades, as the enemy. Something to be fought and conquered rather than as a rich and beautiful watery wilderness deserving of admiration and protection. In fact, many early visitors turned around and left to never return. But not all. Gradually, the tide turned and the migration southward down the peninsula began in earnest after the turn of the century. It has been unrelenting ever since.

Business Begins

CAXAMBAS

On the southern edge of Marco Island sits Caxambas, which, translated from the Native American vernacular, means "fresh water," or translated from Spanish, *cacimba* "a place of wells." The two artesian wells provided potable water to Spanish sailors beginning in the 1700s and later for a new business, one of the first in southwest Florida.

The James Barfield family, having moved to Caxambas in 1892 and opening a general store and hotel, donated five acres in 1904 along what is now Caxambas Pass between the south tip of Marco Island and the Kice islands complex to the E. S. Burnham Packing Company for docks and a processing facility. Canning oysters and clams, the company provided housing for workers and stabilized the island's economy, paying ten cents an hour.

Harvesting clams was hard work until 1908 when Capt. Bill Collier invented a motorized device that scraped the sea bottom with only minor damage to the shells. The clams, described as the size of "softballs," were cleaned and packaged for shipping to northern markets.[22] Hand digging, necessary in shallow water, could produce about 15 bushels per day while the mechanical dredge, operating 24 hours a day, could do over 300 bushels.

Seven years later the Doxsee Clam Factory opened for business. Noted for its clam juice called *"Nature's Tonic"* the facility employed 50 people and enjoyed wide acceptance and distribution of its main product. The Doxsee family had operations from Long Island down the east coast and is still in business today, although not in Florida.

The Burnham Company did not survive the first months of the Great Depression and closed in 1929. The Doxsee Company, left with no competition, lasted until 1948 when the Atlantic Coast Line terminated rail service to Marco Island. The only remnant is noted today in nautical charts as Clam Factory Shoal just east of Henry Key in Caxambas Pass.

While the coastal Glades people and Calusa harvested millions of clams to consume and build mounds, their method of hand harvesting never threatened the sustainability of the mollusks, mechanical dredging had much the same effect on oysters and clams as the plume hunters did on wading birds. It decimated the population and destroyed much of the habitat where clams reproduce and grow. To add to the burden, by the mid-1930s there were over 100 fish houses from Cape Sable north to

Chokoloskee, all seeking to process whatever fishermen could catch and bring to their docks, but only the one clam processing plant. Like the birds, the clams and oysters came back in smaller numbers, being blessed with the productive coastal environment of Southwest Florida.

MANETTA COMPANY

One of the most curious businesses to briefly operate on southwest Florida's lower coast was the Manetta Company. Tannic acid had medicinal uses but in the early 20th century its product was used mainly to cure animal hides for industrial belts on drive shafts powering the machines and looms in textile mills and industrial plants of the northeast. Manetta had been engaged in extraction of tannic acid from mangroves beginning in 1904, but as the supply along the east coast had become exhausted as the thin fringe had been either stripped of bark or excavated for development, it moved operations to southwest Florida. Going down the coast to find abundant mangrove forests, the most southern river to drain the Everglades was the Shark River emptying into Ponce de Leon Bay where the company operated an extraction dredge built on a large platform with worker housing and processing sheds that required constant maintenance. A massive 1910 hurricane destroyed the floating platform and facility used to peel bark, but the company rebuilt the facility and production resumed as World War I increased the demand for leather goods.

After the war, with reduced demand for its product, Manetta decided the mangrove might be used as a building material. A series of experiments were fraught with problems and besides, there was another source of lumber, both cheaper and more widely available: abundant pine forests further north. Faced with low cost competition, the company ceased operations in 1923.

The brief history of the Manetta Company in order of magnitude was insignificant. Only four or five people were employed when it was shuttered. But reduced demand was only part of the story. The other was intervention into the historic sheet flow of water in South Florida. The Shark River is wide and flat but with new private canals being built over fifty miles away, a lowered water table was created, the salt line was moving upstream, and a reliable source of fresh water was gradually drying up.

DEEP LAKE

By the turn of the century, the Florida land boom was in full swing. Railroad magnates, Henry Flagler on the east coast and Henry Plant on the west, punched their way south to Miami and Tampa, they built magnificent hotels and promoted vacations to tourists in major northeastern cities.With increased access and reliable transportation, speculation was rampant.

Enthusiastic about new business opportunities, and with the citrus industry in the northern part of Florida having been decimated by the freeze of 1894-95, John

Roach, owner of a hotel on Useppa Island, and his partner Walter Langford, purchased 300 acres in 1902 around a large sinkhole north and east of Everglade—known because of its depth as Deep Lake. Roach owned the Chicago Street Railway Company and was convinced that south Florida had a future laden with profits from the right enterprises. The lake was slightly less than 2 acres in size but over 95 feet deep, and with salt water being slightly heavier than fresh, there was a lens on the surface of the lake that could be used for both cultivation and drinking water. Seminole Chief Billy Bowlegs had settled there in the 1840s for exactly that reason. After clearing adjacent land by mechanical means, the partners planted a variety of trees perfectly adapted to Florida's environment and were able to produce seedless fruit. Trees had to be brought in from Fort Myers by boat then hauled to the grove by oxcart, and the fruit back for delivery to either Fort Myers or Key West the same way. After seven years of operation, a hurricane in 1910 destroyed the season's crop, but did little damage to the enthusiasm of Roach and Langford who decided that they needed a short line railroad to expedite movement of equipment and crops to and from Everglade.

Roach brought his friend Barron Collier in as a partner on the rail line, and in 1913 laid fourteen miles of narrow gauge track. Flatbed cars were pulled by an engine jury-rigged with a Ford motor but could only function when the weather cooperated because the rail bed flooded during heavy storms. Despite the obstacles, in 1915 they delivered 15,000 boxes of grapefruit to Fort Myers.

Langford died in 1921. Roach then sold Deep Lake to Collier in 1922 for a hunting lodge and resort. Collier, always looking beyond the immediate to expand his businesses, began to seek ways to expand rail service and in 1928, upon completion of the Tamiami Trail, sold the rail right-of-way to the Atlantic Coast Line as part of a deal to bring passenger and freight service to Everglades City.

CROSS FLORIDA HIGHWAY

Before World War I, while Plant and Flagler were building railroads down both coasts, businessmen were talking about linking the two sides of the state with the Cross-Florida Barge Canal. But construction on the waterway started in 1935. The canal was to be 230 miles long and would drain the Ocklawaha River just southeast of Ocala. The project bumped along until World War II halted construction. Later, in the 1960s Pres. John Kennedy and Lyndon Johnson joined with Florida Gov. Ferris Bryant (D-FL) to resurrect the canal. Construction began again in 1964, but by 1969 a group of environmentalists, under the banner of Florida Defenders of the Environment (FDE) brought suit. Using tactics that would become the model for challenging a large jetport being constructed in the Big Cypress, they gathered significant national media attention to the project which was halted by Pres. Richard Nixon in 1971.

Well before the canal, plans were afoot to link the east coast to Tampa by a road as the automobile and truck replaced transport by boat. The main impetus came from Miami, and a route south of Lake Okeechobee was selected as preferable to one north through the Kissimmee Lakes wetlands. As the plans became public, communities on the west coast objected because it would leave Immokalee, a major farm product distribution center, in the lurch because the connection from communities south of Fort Myers was nothing more than a sand trail, usable only in good weather but no small town wanted to be left out, sponsoring formation of a multitude of Road and Bridge Districts with bonding power to raise the funds necessary to bring the highway through their towns. Immokalee, Marco Island and Naples were all caught up in the frenzy but had a low tax base, so when cost estimates were developed reality set in. A bit surprising because standards for building highways at the time were almost nonexistent; a slightly weather-resistant flat surface would suffice. By 1914, each community raised enough money to build a portion of the road, and after lengthy negotiations it was decided that it would bend east near Marco Island.

Construction began in 1915 and continued in fits and starts. The idea was to begin on both coasts and work toward the center of the state using the standard dredge and fill technique where the subsurface would be formed by digging up muck and mounding it to form a base, with the ditch creating a borrow canal to handle water immediately alongside the right-of-way.

Early segments in the western section were tough going. There was little rock but a lot of messy work in what was described as:

> "... truly jungle in every sense of the word—a mass of trees of all kinds and sizes thousands of switches, poles, brush, ferns all woven together with bamboo rattan and vines. Perhaps several hundred would be chopped off the ground before the mass would fall, so that it could be chipped apart with brush axes. It was scrub and mangrove and grass muck. Think of leaves on the trees shaking and trembling in the whole mass of muck and sand hundreds of feet in each direction quivering and shaking like a mass of jelly with each by vibration of the dredge engine. Then think of putting a 40,000 pound engine across it ... with muck and marl twelve feet deep and chancing the slightest mistake or error of judgment it would make a buried and tangled wreck of 40,000 pounds of steel and machinery." [23]

Efforts on the east coast ran into some of the same problems but to a lesser extent and by 1918 over 40 miles had been completed from the Dade County terminus.

Part of the success was because the Florida legislature, concerned with the lack of progress in draining wetlands, had passed a law in 1913 allowing developers to create their own drainage districts. By 1917 there were four canals running from Lake Okeechobee to the growing cities of Miami, Fort Lauderdale and Boca Raton, so the land was a little drier.

Road building techniques through a swamp improved over time, but the results were still pretty shabby. The initial stretch financed by west coast interests had not reached Carnestown by 1918, and what had been put down was not wide enough in some places for two cars to pass. To save on materials, bridges were built too low and kept getting washed out by rainstorms. Project backers, having to continually repair the damage, kept running out of money.

When the United States entered World War I, materials became more expensive and less available. Lee County interests ran out of money and construction on the road was shut down. But to the rescue from the east came James Jaudon. His Chevelier Corporation had purchased over 200,000 acres in Monroe County and if Lee County would agree to run the road down through his property, he promised to finance and finish building it.[24]

Starting construction in 1921 Jaudon established a town along the road called Pinecrest, advertising it as the "Next Miami" with a large community center and hundreds, if not thousands, of houses, hotels and a casino.[25]

The Florida land boom was in full swing again after the war, but despite the heady promises Jaudon ran out of money in 1923 just when Barron Collier stepped into the picture.

BARRON COLLIER AND THE TRAIL

Barron Gift Collier was born in Memphis Tennessee. Quitting school at sixteen, he conceived the idea of strategically placed advertisements above the shelving in New York City trolley cars to capture the attention of riders who had little else to look at, and at the age of 27 owned the Consolidated Street Railway Advertising Company. He began visiting Useppa Island in Charlotte Harbor around 1911 and purchased the island's hotel from his host John Roach, who was at the time president of the Chicago Street Railway Company. The more Collier traveled around southwest Florida the more he saw as potential for development. The question was: where and how?

To answer the question with an unusual twist of fate, in April 1923, with railroads, highways and developments burgeoning along both coasts, a small group called the "Trail Blazers" decided to drive from Fort Myers to Miami along the original route proposed passing through the Jaudon property—even though there was a 30 mile gap where construction had stopped. Promoters of the trail and lovers of the Model "T" Ford motorcar, they attempted to reinvigorate interest and took two Indians to guide them through the swamp. With 10 cars they kept bogging down until they reached a point there were no more obvious trails. The guides reconnoitered, located surveyor stakes in modern-day Monroe County and headed east into uncharted territory. Running out of both gas and food, they sent members to Miami to report on progress and to bring back needed supplies to the main party. They slipped and slogged through the final miles on foot leaving cars to be pulled out by tractors. The trip with attendant ballyhoo was celebrated as a resounding success, as much for the Trail as for Fort Myers winter resident Henry Ford and his new Model "T."

Having been heavily reported by the national news media, it might also have persuaded Collier to finish the road, because in May 1923 he approached the Internal Improvement Fund with a proposal to purchase state-owned land in south Lee County. He had already acquired large tracts from timber companies, but felt a need to consolidate. The Fund, always eager to turn land into cash, agreed. However they had one condition: that Collier finish the partially built road to be known as the Tamiami Trail. In return he imposed his single condition: that the land he purchased would be incorporated into a new county of 1.3 million acres and be named for him. By the time he finished, Collier owned 900,000 of those acres.

Returning to the Fund a year later after carefully studying proposed alternatives, he insisted that the road go further north, along an alternative route in Collier County, and not south through the Jaudon holdings in Monroe

County. The Miami crowd, having backed Jaudon and Chevelier, were opposed but unable to finance finishing the Loop Road, so the state accepted Collier's terms even though there was almost 60 new miles to excavate.

With operations based in Everglades City, which at Collier's insistence had become the new county seat, he built a dock and equipment storage area called Port DuPont, to move men and equipment into the construction zone and hired Graham Copeland, a capable engineer, to build the road.

Copeland used a machine known as the Bay City walking dredge, a monstrous device resembling a giant metal stork straddling the canal and biting into the substrate with a small three foot bucket. While moving through swampland the behemoth would establish a base of sand and muck down the center survey line and 30 feet across to be the width of the roadbed. Base with limestone and hard rock would then be laid about four feet above grade. Progress averaged about 160 feet per day with two dredges working around the clock, stopping only for repairs.[26]

Copeland continued to improve the quality of the roadbed. For the first miles, the substrate consisted mainly of marl and sand, but the dredges soon encountered a problem: two miles east of Carnestown the fill material turned into solid rock. In the stretch from there to Dade County, three million sticks of dynamite were used to blow out the rock, and at the dedication ceremony, it was pointed

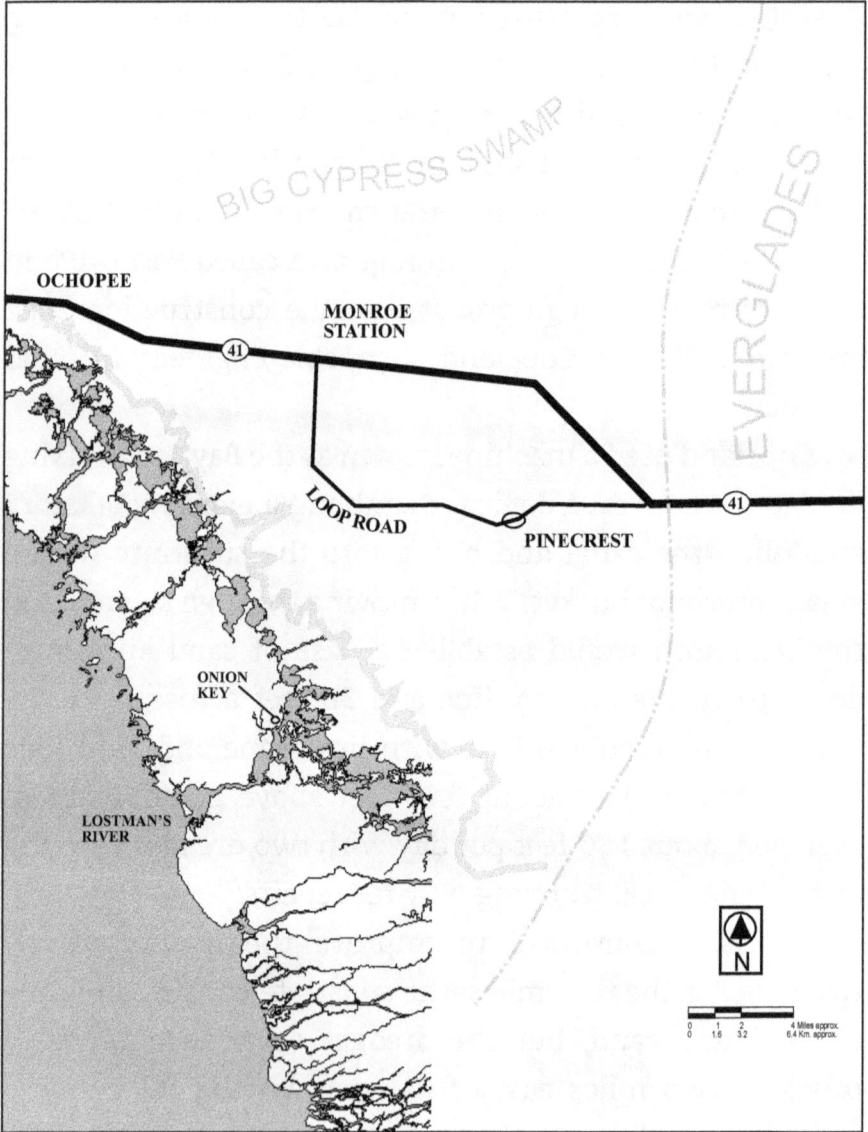

Tamiami Trail and the Loop Road.
Map created by John G. Beriault.

out that "...if the dynamite were laid end to end it would reach from Jacksonville to San Francisco, California." [27]

The road was built perpendicular to the sheet flow of the Big Cypress. The borrow canal was on the upstream side to control and direct water into culverts and under bridges. Had it been built on the downstream side, it would have spread the water more evenly but risked inundating the road during heavy rainstorms.

The Trail was opened on April 25, 1928, almost 13 years after construction had begun. The ribbon cutting was an occasion populated by luminaries and politicians, marked by long speeches, gaiety and celebration.

What had happened, and what was not talked about at the time, was that the Tamiami Trail, and to a lesser degree the Loop Road, were basically dams built across the Big Cypress Swamp. In places where it clearly needed to be bridged, like at river crossings, water was allowed to flow beneath the road. In other areas a limited number of culverts were built, effectively compressing the flow of water into a narrow funnel rather than allowing it to spread naturally along the surface of the land and gradually percolate into the soil and surface aquifers.

The Trail and Loop Roads also cut off a number of canoe channels used by the Seminoles. As mechanized transport began to take over, this became less important except as a reminder of the changes that road construction was placing not only on the landscape but also on the humans who once occupied it. The Miccosukee were most affected. Separated from the Seminoles and recognized as an independent Tribe in 1962, they had existed as part of the Seminole nation in the Big Cypress raising crops and cattle, left alone by the increasing number of White settlers because there was little to offer in the swamp except seclusion until the road builders came. The Miccosukee would later adapt by building businesses for the tourist trade, and while property rights is historically one of the fundamental underpinnings of Florida culture and law, the rules were clearly applied selectively as the native population had its land appropriated by the state time and time again.

But the Trail was not the end of road building for Barron Collier. His headquarters and the county seat, at the newly named Everglades City, needed north-south access through the Big Cypress for development that Collier believed was soon to come. It would connect to Immokalee, a vibrant farming community. Now designated as State Route 29 it separates the Big Cypress from the present-day Fakahatchee Strand and Florida Panther Refuge on the west side of the road. How it came to be illustrates Collier's great desire to build infrastructure to serve what he saw as a growing opportunity in southwest Florida.

SR 29 AND THE ATLANTIC COAST LINE

In addition to a road, Collier needed rail service. His grove at Deep Lake was connected by a short line to Everglades City. From there, produce would go by boat to

Fort Myers for packaging and distribution. But mainline rail offered less packing and unpacking time and more competitive rates so Collier hired Sam Thompson, who had engineered the Deep Lake connection, to build both road and elevated rail bed simultaneously. The road would serve a number of burgeoning small businesses and the ACL tracks provided reliable and easy transport to Tampa for passengers as well as shipping for large farms growing tomatoes and other row crops around Immokalee.

The ACL was willing to run track to the new spur. It had been building a line from Haines City south since 1910, after acquiring the Moore Haven and Clewiston Railway. Since 1921, it had the large Southern Sugar Corporation as its main customer, and was looking for more agribusiness shipping in south Florida. It found an opportunity in the Fort Myers Southern Railroad, chartered in 1918 to a small group of investors. Running short of money they allowed the charter to lapse until 1925 when they leased it to the ACL for tracks from Fort Myers to Marco Island.

Thompson's main dredge was gigantic, a nearly four-ton monster with outriggers to keep it stable. The boom reached out 110 feet. Sleeping quarters for eight people was on a nearby floating barge.[28] The work went on twenty-four hours a day, with the behemoth starting in Immokalee and a smaller dredge moving north from just south of Miles City. The borrow canal was anywhere between 30 and 60 feet wide and 6 to 12 feet deep.[29]

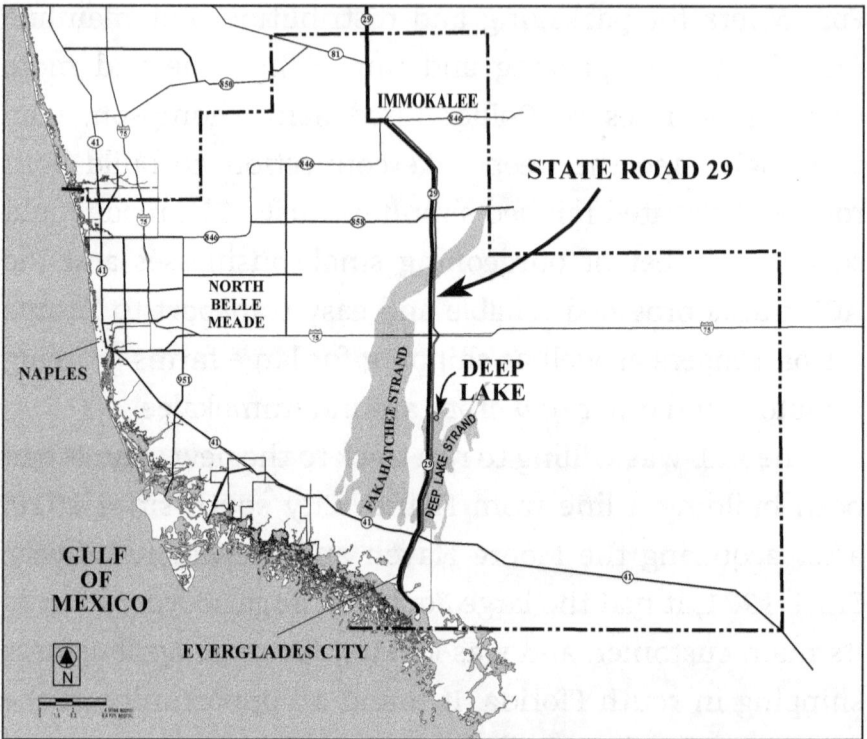

State Road 29, canal and Deep Lake.
Map created by John G. Beriault.

Excavated along the eastern side of the road, it intercepted sheet flow from Hendry County down to the coast near Everglades City. Underpasses and drainage weirs were designed to move water from the borrow canal beneath the road and rail bed from east to west, but limited in number, very small and utterly inadequate because most of the road was built parallel, not perpendicular, to the prevailing flow at the time. Some water during heavy rainfall escaped into adjacent strands and small ponds reducing the hydrologic pressure to move water through the underpasses.

The SR 29 builders had the additional problem of building trestles capable of handling heavy locomotives and loaded freight cars. ACL tracks ran alongside the road, until they turned east to connect with Deep Lake short line, because part of Collier's deal was that trains would end up at a charming stucco passenger terminal in Everglades City. Opening in June 1928, the first Pullmans unloaded curious tourists anxious to see the natural wonders that awaited them, with the possibility of finding the perfect lot for a retirement home or fishing camp to the delight of Mr. Collier.

The story of Deep Lake and SR 29 is significant, because it produced three outcomes leading to the eventual near destruction of the Big Cypress drainage basin. First, the SR 29 road and rail bed impeded the sheet flow of the original system. Second, it emphasized the importance of land transportation. Prior to Deep Lake, the movement of goods was by either oxcart or water. Cargo ships plying Florida's coast had little or no effect on the land, but with the introduction of rail service and roads that would all change. Third, with Barron Collier's influence and nose for business opportunities, it brought a new perspective and new money into southwest Florida.

POINCIANA

Opening of the Tamiami Trail from the east created an opportunity for Miami promoters. On the coast near the mouth of Lostman's River sat Onion Key, a small but high island. It was headquarters for the Tropical Development Company's sales and marketing for a 9,000 home subdivision with a small commercial plaza platted in 1925 along the north shore of the river. It was called Poinciana. Heavily promoted as "Miami of the Gulf," visitors had to drive across the completed eastern part of the Trail to the new town of Pinecrest. From there, they would walk six miles to a landing at the headwaters of Lostman's River to be delivered downstream by boat to the development site.

Realizing that just getting there was a problem, the company produced sales maps showing plans for a new road called the Poinciana Trail running from the Loop Road directly to the new town. A second proposed road, called the Cape Sable Loop Highway, was shown running down the southern edge of Dade and Monroe County, turning north at Cape Sable and ending up in Poinciana after crossing miles of coastal mangrove forests.

South Florida had been devastated by a major hurricane in 1910, and weather settled down for the next fifteen years. But memories were short and optimism long. Poinciana sold over 6,500 lots in its first year. The lots were 50 feet deep and sold for $100 with a corner lot priced at $250.[30] Then, on September 18, 1926 a storm hit the east coast and moved west. It killed almost 300 people and wiped out Clewiston. Known as the Great Miami Hurricane, storm surge was eight feet at Everglades City washing into the town and forcing people to seek shelter on the second story of the only two-story building: the Everglades Inn. Houses were flattened by the wind; the detritus was blown into the raging Gulf. It wiped out Onion Key. Poinciana promoters vowed to carry on, but buyers began to lose interest.

A second storm hit in 1928. Known as the Okeechobee Hurricane, it killed over 2,500 people and flooded both Pahokee and Belle Glade. Port DuPont, the area set aside to receive materials for Tamiami Trail construction, was leveled. The Collier interests remained undaunted and rebuilt the facility. The devastation brought President Herbert Hoover, a trained engineer, down to Florida where he quickly appropriated federal funds to build what would become an eponymously named earthen levee around the lake to protect the small communities to the south.

With the second storm, Poinciana was toast, but its legacy was destined to last for many years. When the National Park Service was working on land acquisition for Everglades National Park, a few real estate title problems arose because of the inadequacy or absence of records that had been destroyed on Onion Key in the hurricanes of 1926 and 1928.

UNWELCOME VISITORS

If the storms had not daunted fickle tourists and optimistic developers, a little flying insect added to their misery. An invasion of the Mediterranean fruit fly, known better as the Medfly, with remarkable reproduction rates boosted by floods and high water, first appeared in a grapefruit grove near Orlando. As the bugs spread President Hoover, familiar with problems in south Florida, put the full force of the federal government behind sequestering the outbreak. National Guard troops set up check points at highways in and out of the state in an all-out attempt to stop the spread.

Capable of attacking over 260 varieties of fruits, nuts and vegetables, the flies eventually infected 67% of the fruit trees extending over 8 million acres. Eradication cost $7.5 million; the loss of tourist dollars was incalculable. But the Medfly was not the main reason development in Florida came to a grinding halt because in October 1929 the nation entered into a long slide known as the Great Depression.

Resource Extraction

LOGGING INDUSTRY

In 1845, when Florida achieved statehood, there were over 25 million acres of timber in the state. Logging was, for the next century, an enduring economic engine despite time and money spent to drain the Everglades to grow sugar and row crops and rooftops.

The history of logging companies is marked by a dazzling array of interlocking ownership, cooperative working agreements, purchases and mergers. An original was the J. C. Turner Cypress Company. In 1913 it paid $1.4 million for 150,000 acres of timber rights in Lee and Collier counties. The company owned 40% of the operation, and was knowledgeable in handling the large, heavy trees, having been formed in 1895 to log cypress in both Louisiana and Florida. A second company, Burton-Schwartz, owned the other 60%, and had built a cypress sawmill in Taylor County. The Carpenter-O'Brien Company owned 48% of Burton-Schwartz and operated a pine sawmill in Eastport, near Jacksonville.

But the elephant in the room was the Brooks-Scanlon Company from Minneapolis, a voracious acquirer of land. By 1920 it owned 900,000 acres of timber, making it the largest property owner in Florida at the time. Eventually it bought out Carpenter-O'Brien and ran the Eastport mill until 1929, when it closed the facility and moved to Foley, building a company town with a population of over 3,000 souls and a new mill—the largest in the state.

A smaller company was run by Immokalee resident C. J. Jones, who began logging in the late 1930s after building a pine sawmill operation near the rail line running along SR 29. Most of the logging was done north and east of the town where it was easier to move logs on firm ground using bulldozers. The only operator in southwest Florida to do finished lumber at a local mill, and capable of doing 40,000 board feet per day, Jones built the company town of Jerome with a church and housing for the workers.[31]

By the 1930s pine forests in north and central Florida were logged out and with the opening of the Tamiami Trail and ACL rail service to Everglades City, south Florida was becoming more accessible for logging, but demand for building materials was limited because the Great Depression ravaged the industry. The Jones Company was beginning to falter and Burton-Schwartz sold their operations to the Lee Cypress Company, a holding company formed in 1924 to own the J. C Turner Cypress Company which, after the war, became the Lee Tidewater Cypress Company, a single business entity from the remnants of the four original loggers.[32]

Then, World War II changed the fortunes of the loggers. When the Japanese bombed naval facilities in Pearl Harbor demand for cypress, being used for packing crates and barrels and coffins, soared. And in south Florida lumbermen found the bald cypress, with some trees having grown for over 600 years, measuring up to 25 feet around and soaring 130 feet high. The trees could be cut into large boards, especially useful for ship building because the cypress was rot resistant and durable. Because of its size, it was hard to cut and even harder to move to the mills but highly desirable with the greatest military need coming from the United States Navy and its growing fleet of minesweepers. Cypress lacked the magnetic signature of steel, so was ideal for searching out floating explosives that would detonate when approached by a steel hull. At the peak of operations, Florida was generating over one million board feet of cypress every week.

Logging in the Fakahatchee and Big Cypress was dangerous. The work environment was replete with snakes and saw grass and deep water creating rashes on the sawyer's feet and legs. Because of the size of trees, equipment used was massive. In a moment of inattention or with the slip of the hand, disaster could strike. To pull the giant trees out of the swamp temporary tracks were laid on trams. The trees, once felled, were cut into a size that would fit onto railcars, then picked up by a crane cabled to a tree to immobilize it, then lowered, guided by workers, onto flat cars in a process called "skidding."

The skidder crew in the forest would cut logs into 40-foot lengths, then either use a gas powered vehicle to drag the logs out or put them on a tram car pulled by a "lokey" to send them to be loaded onto railroad flat cars on the ACL main line. The sawyers, or bushmen, were paid by the foot for this work.

The roadbed for the trams was usually built using the technique of a shallow borrow canal with the excavated sand and muck supporting the crossties. Sometimes, in cases where the line was very short, cypress ties and rails were simply laid at grade and taken up and moved as soon as the area was logged out. As forests were thinned to the point where it was increasingly expensive to get trees out and delivered to sawmills. Railroad engines and cars were sold, tracks were removed, and the roadbeds left intact to become paths through the desecrated wilderness.

After World War II, the Florida timber industry began to regenerate its pinewood forests. The preferred method was by mechanized planting of seedlings in sites with compatible soil, but cypress regeneration was more difficult. Because of the water depths mechanical means was not a viable alternative. Cypress seeds required months of soaking prior to germination and many parts of the swamp, being inundated during the wet season, would dry out in the fall and winter. The cypress was a slow-growing species and to reach a size economically profitable for harvest could take as much as 100 growing years whereas slash pines took only 20 years to produce decent timber.

With good engineering, hydrology could be restored to some extent, so the real damage was done to the plants and animals dependent upon wooded areas to survive and thrive. When trees were felled, it opened the canopy allowing exotic species to gain purchase in the watershed. This was particularly true of exotic melaleuca, originally introduced in 1906 by John Gifford as a way to stabilize coastlines and dry out the Everglades. It spread quickly to invade swampy areas once populated by cypress trees. As the exotics competed with native species the entire ecosystem, including sites of food sources for wood storks, changed forever. In addition the trams or elevated roadbeds were colonized by upland species such as tropical hardwoods and non-wetland dependent flora. Climax vegetation, established in Darwinian fashion over the centuries, was strongly resistant to invaders but as deforestation took place over a short period of time the system became unbalanced and susceptible.

Plant life was not the only part of the biota to suffer. There is a strong possibility that two bird species, the Carolina Parakeet and the Ivory-billed woodpecker, may have become extinct due to logging the Big Cypress and upland pine forests and the Red Cockaded woodpecker became endangered as it was deprived of the old trees it used for nesting.

OIL IN THE BIG CYPRESS

In the early years of the 20th century, the search for oil in Florida had been centered in the northern part of the state along the Panhandle. The results were mixed. Near the town of Pensacola two wells were drilled at 1,600 and 1,700 feet. Excitement mounted initially but the wells were soon capped. False alarm.

The Lee Tidewater Cypress Company was interested in drilling for oil but held ownership and leases only to the surface of the land. Barron Collier had the mineral rights and once he completed the Tamiami Trail in 1928, he negotiated a lease with Gulf Oil. The company tried several test wells as far down as 6,000 feet. All were dry holes. After further seismic testing the company concluded that drilling in Collier County would not be profitable and departed in 1938, a year before Collier passed away.

Undaunted by Gulf's failure another driller, Peninsular Oil and Refining, sunk a well close to the nearly abandoned village of Pinecrest in 1939 to 10,000 feet. Coring showed promise, but the well failed to produce, and the company decided it did not need another dry hole.

As the automobile became ubiquitous in American society demand for petroleum soared and in order to stir interest in 1941, just before Pearl Harbor, the governor and cabinet offered a bounty of $50,000 for the first company to drill a working well in Florida.

With the war effort driving the country's economy, 129 test holes were drilled unsuccessfully until 1943 when the first well to go into full production in the Big Cypress was brought in by the Loffland Brothers from Tulsa, Oklahoma under contract with the Humble Oil Company. The site lay 12 miles south of Immokalee. Initially producing 97 barrels, it eventually got up to 140 barrels per day of oil with 425 gallons of salt water. As the well continued to produce, salt water was gradually reduced to 20 gallons a day.

The oil came from the Sunniland Trend, 150 miles long and approximately 20 miles wide running from Miami northwest to Fort Myers and then nearly 200 miles out into the Gulf of Mexico. The productive zone lay between 9,500 to 12,000 feet below the surface. Sunniland wells by 1954 were producing 21,000 barrels a month from an average depth of 11,575 feet.[33] Creating more impetus to drill in Florida, the National Petroleum Council issued a report in 1972 indicating that beneath the peninsula and out on the continental shelf, there could be as much as 7.8 billion barrels of crude, but the projection turned out to be somewhat hyperbolic. Franklin Adams recalls:

During the early days of the oil seismic and drilling activities there was little concern as the search was viewed as economically beneficial to the private mineral rights owners and the oil companies. That would eventually change as the public became more aware of the surface damage occurring in what in the early days was a mostly unregulated industry. In response to concerns from the public and environmental organizations in 1971 Gov. Askew established the Big Cypress Swamp Advisory Committee.

With the Petroleum Council's optimistic projection, the trend was drilled later at Bear Island, at the northwest tip of the Big Cypress National Preserve in 1972 and at Raccoon Point near the Dade/Collier county line in 1978, before the preserve was created. Adams again:

In 1972 the Florida Department of Natural Resources established regulations on permitting requirements in Florida. They became the most stringent of any state in the U. S. But enforcement and monitoring in this large watershed region was difficult, and not a priority for some.

By 1978, with drilling at Raccoon Point, the recoverable reserve in southwest Florida was estimated at 38 million barrels.[34] In context, the United States produces over 10 million barrels per day. Oil from the Sunniland averages about 2,800 barrels per day.

Today, oil from the Big Cypress must be pumped from the well to a tank farm where the crude and salt water are separated, then through a series of transfer pumps until it reaches Port Everglades. From there it is barged to refineries in Texas. The oil itself is fairly sweet with relatively low sulfur content, but transportation adds to the expense of bringing oil out of the Big Cypress. The overall impact of exploration and drilling seems to have had little impact because of well-defined rules governing oil production. More damage has been done by highway development than by drilling.

In the future, any problems would most likely come from the injection of acidic chemicals to stimulate new channels in the limestone to allow oil to flow more freely. Since the technique is new, and has been used in a different geological setting, the long-term effects are unknown and it would be a shame to use extraction techniques better suited for shale than in the carbonate rock and marl substrate of a national preserve.

Environmental Awakening

Ever since the failure of Napoleon Bonaparte Broward's "Empire of the Everglades," Florida has looked for ways to grow its economy and job base beyond timber and agriculture. The burgeoning cities of the east coast provided jobs for construction workers, and rails being laid on both sides of the state gave the promise of reliable transportation for people and movement of goods. But there was always another summer and in some cases, another monster hurricane.

Natural resources in the Big Cypress, above and under ground, had been exploited by generations for human benefit and profit, but there was another paradigm coming into play after World War II, beginning with a book in 1962 titled *Silent Spring.* While Rachel Carson's book had nothing to do with logging or oil, it made people look a little harder at how nature was being manipulated by chemicals with the possibility of unintended consequences. It also gave rise to the environmental movement in the United States, and coincided with an effort in Florida to build a massive airport in the middle of nowhere.

A tale of the Big Cypress jetport and other stories that follow describe a series of separate events during different periods of time playing out with different characters, using their skills and influence to place vast expanses of land into conservation easements and public ownership. There is some temporal overlapping and there are projects still ongoing after decades of effort, due mainly to lack of money but not a lack of determination. It is to those stories that we now turn.

C&SF PROJECT

A series of storm systems in the summer of 1947 dumped over 100 inches of rain on southeast Florida. The few private canals at the time were unable to handle the volume and Miami was inundated.

I remember the 1947 storms and rain well. It was one of the most exciting times for a ten-year-old boy who seemed unaware of the tremendous property damage caused by this hurricane. Water was pouring out of the Glades down the Miami River and the tidal waters of Biscayne Bay were pushing up the river against the tremendous flow out of the Glades. It was bound to flood. My father and I remained at home during the storm but the rest of our family left to shelter at Miami High School. During the night the river rose and by daylight had risen to two feet in our downstairs living room. The old Persian rug which had floated in the 1926 and 1935 hurricanes was floating once again. It made for difficult walking. Pushing the front door open at daylight, I will never forget the sight before me. Torn, twisted and downed trees were everywhere. A large boat rested at the front of our property where it had been driven from the river. The silence was incredible. All electrical power was out and Miami was at a standstill. For several days, my friends and I took home found treasures blown by the wind and carried by the waters. It was an exciting time for kids and a time of considerable work for the adults.

A more comprehensive water management system was needed with the emphasis on flood control. All water districts were consolidated into a single unit and the Congress appropriated funds in 1948 for the U. S. Army Corps of Engineers to do something substantial and quickly. As a first step the Corps created a 100 mile long perimeter levee running down the Atlantic Coastal Ridge to protect most of western Palm Beach, Broward and Miami-Dade counties and the cities of Fort Lauderdale and Miami from inundation. The levee ran down as far as Homestead to block flow to the east and protect other smaller communities from flooding.

Over 1,000 additional miles of canals followed, with pump stations to redirect water where and when needed. While only indirectly affecting the southwest part of the state, the Central and South Florida Project for Flood Control and Other Purposes (C&SF) had two main objectives with the first being to provide water for rapidly urbanizing areas on the east coast and recharge the Biscayne Aquifer—the main source of potable water for southeast Florida. Aquifers depended upon percolation and the slow absorption of flowing surface water to achieve a balance with a levee and canal system designed to sequester and move water fast. The Corps created three Water Conservation Areas (WCAs), designed to be filled during rainy season and pumped out when necessary. The first and northernmost was WCA-1. It became the Arthur Marshall Loxahatchee National Wildlife Refuge and encompassed most of the Hillsborough Lakes area. The next one was WCA-2 and linked just to the south and east of the Big Cypress was WCA-3 covering a total of 915 sq. mi. The largest portion was in Broward and Miami-Dade counties at 786 sq. mi. designated as WCA-3A with a large gap to allow water to flow from Mullet Slough into the Big Cypress for aquifer recharge and to help hydrate the Park. If the Corps could engineer a system to control the storage and release of water and mimic seasonal patterns,

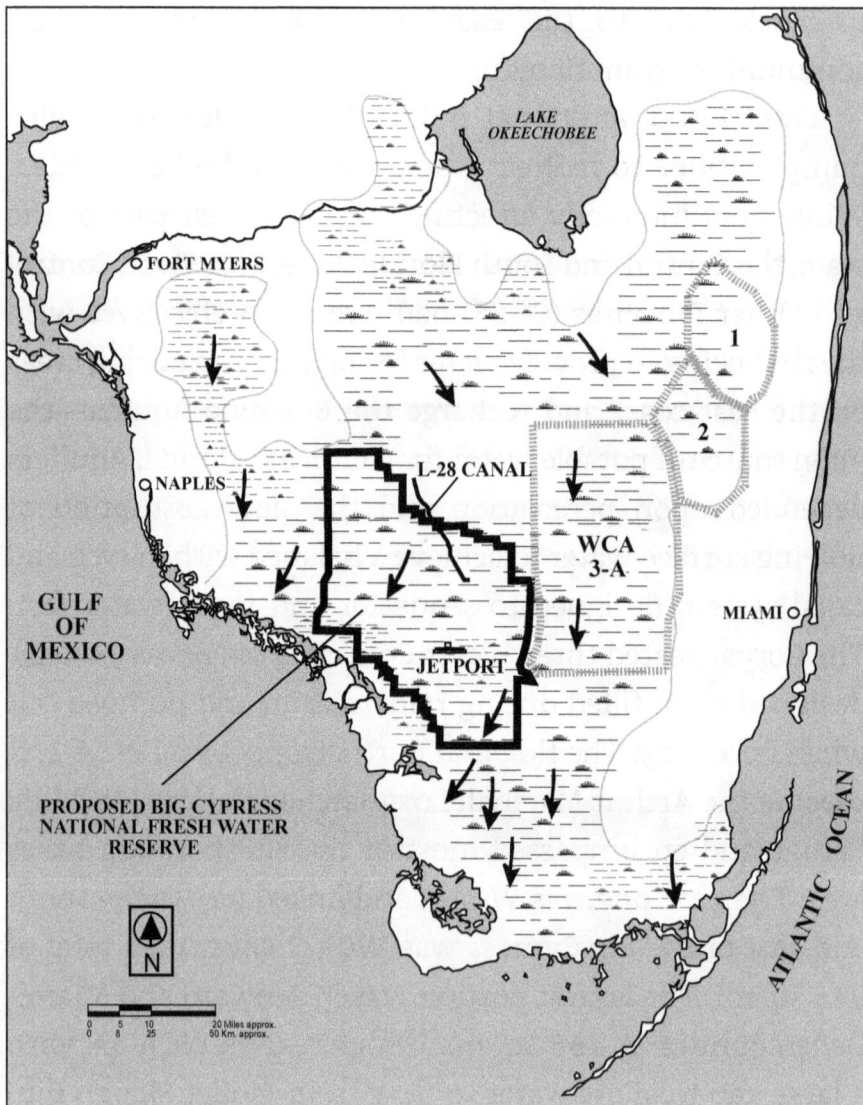

CS&F Project including L-28 and WCA-3 with Jetport location.
Map created by John G. Beriault.

it might just save the Everglades—drying out since the days of Hamilton Disston.

The second objective was the "Other Purposes" of the C&SF act: to drain as much land as possible for agriculture and development south of Lake Okeechobee by creating a gigantic farming complex called the Everglades Agricultural Area (EAA) that could be irrigated by pumping water from the lake into farm fields when needed and back again when not. Since the EAA was directly north of Everglades National Park, it became completely dependent upon water managers for survival.

Further west, C&SF engineers were planning to build a canal and levee separating the western Everglades from the central swamp that fed into the EAA.

Canals have three purposes: first, to protect populated areas from flooding; second, to collect and direct water for human use including irrigation; third, to drain land for development. The L-28 levee and canal were designed for the third purpose.

L-28

Since the initial focus of the C&SF project was on the east coast and central Everglades, construction of the L-28 would not begin for 15 years and while the C&SF project was mainly about water, reengineering the landscape provided an opportunity for development in southwest Florida in the form of a massive airport.

In 1963, dredges began tearing up wetlands in Miami-Dade county beginning just past the Monroe County section of the Loop Road where it meets US 41. A nine-mile south-north stretch of levees was completed in 1963, and plans were made to extend north into Broward County where it would turn west. That section, up to the Collier County line, was also begun in 1963 and completed in 1965. But there it stopped.

Collier County surface flow, generally down slope to the south and southwest is determined by underlying geology. Starting at the Immokalee Rise where the elevation is about 30 feet above mean sea level (msl), it oozes gradually down gradient to the Ten Thousand Islands and Everglades National Park. But the passage is not smooth. There are lumps and anomalies, particularly at the border between the central Everglades and what is now the Big Cypress. That ridge, called the Sha-Ha-Lege, creates a geological divide where land is generally higher on the west side than on the east where the WCAs were being constructed.

The problem was apparent. The levee was designed to funnel the water from Collier County into WCA-3A, a large wetland set aside to feed directly into Everglades Park while making eastern Collier County dry enough for development all the way to Naples. Water did flow into the WCA-3A but drained the wrong way in one section due to an irregular contour. To correct the problem, the Corps left a 7.5 mile gap on the northern edge of the first levee, and dug an interceptor canal from above I-75 to help drain water into WCA-3A. The gap was located in the Miccosukee Reservation and the interceptor in the Big Cypress Seminole Reservation. It was, and still is, a point of controversy because much of the water passing through reservation lands is polluted.[35]

The canals and levees dried out much of the land around a site that was planned to become a major transportation hub, a jetport capable of handling the Concorde, a supersonic airliner in the early development phases by Sud Aviation and British Aerospace. Design of the Concorde had begun in 1962 and one of the early assumptions was that the airliner would require long runways for takeoffs and landings. The proposed jetport was eager to handle the traffic.[36]

BIG CYPRESS AIRPORT

The idea of a new airport was made public in the mid-1960s. However much earlier, in 1957, a confidential study had been done to relieve the pressure of training flights in and out of Miami International. Two alternative locations were identified: one near Biscayne Bay and the other somewhere in the Everglades.[37] While there was little reported publicly at the time, it was clear that the Dade County Port Authority (DCPA) was favoring the location to the west.

As plans for the Concorde were made public, the authority paid for a second study which, not surprisingly, recommended the new airport be built just south of the

Tamiami Trail at a site on the north edge of Everglades National Park. The Park Service found out about it and objected strongly based upon noise disrupting visitors and wildlife, so DCPA then moved to a 39 square-mile location north of the Trail and just west of WCA-3A in the Big Cypress swamp. About one third would be located in Dade County, and the other two thirds in Collier County. The final site, six miles north of the Park, 36 miles from Miami and 49 miles from Marco Island, was announced after protracted secret negotiations with the two counties involved.

But according to one source a development of that size would produce 5 million gallons of sewage a day in addition to 25 tons of jet fuel pollutants.[38] Although interdicted by the Tamiami Trail at the new site, water would eventually end up in Everglades National Park. The destruction of the entire ecosystem was a real possibility. Despite unanswered environmental questions, the authority began purchasing land quietly and meeting privately with the C&SF Authority seeking approval for a training airport. There was no discussion at the time of anything larger or grander, and the question was never put: why build an airport in the middle of nowhere and north of one of America's iconic national parks just for pilot training? And the answer was: to a great extent it depended upon the drainage projects undertaken in the area during the previous five years like the L-28, and the real scope of the project was about to be revealed.

JETPORT JUGGERNAUT

It turned out that the port authority had planned for a lot more than just takeoff and landings. In June 1968 the director of the DCPA said: "... five years from now the hotels will be there. A large city will grow up around this jetport. We think it will have aircraft manufacturing plants and even an air college." [39] He believed that a number of businesses would locate, and eventually as many as 150,000 people would be living around the airport, adding to the tax base in Collier County which was one underlying reason for the Dade-Collier agreement.

With things going swimmingly, a groundbreaking ceremony was held on September 18, 1968. Two 10,000 foot runways would be capable of handling the Concorde and other supersonic airliners as well as practice for military and civilian pilots. Connections to Miami and the west coast of Florida would be by either I-75 or a high speed train traveling as much as 200 mph on a cushion of air. The little town of Ochopee on the Trail was booming. A new trailer park and land sales offices were opening up, but despite the boosterish atmosphere at the dedication one speaker, Chief Buffalo Tiger, Chair of the Miccosukee Tribe, commented: "Indians have always given way, moving away from progress in search of peace and quiet, but now there is no place to go." [40]

He was right. Bulldozers and dredges were noisily removing earth from wetland areas to build the first runway when Robert Padrick, the chair of the Central and

Southern Florida Flood Control District, learned that the proposed routing of the upgraded I-75 would go through WCA-3A, a designated wildlife refuge. In a letter to the State Road Department, he registered a strong objection but was told that alignment and positioning of interchanges to the limited access interstate was done by the DCPA and the state roads agency. Secrecy and misrepresentation surrounding routing of the highway caused an uproar not just in the District but also among conservation groups because Padrick had sent a copy of his letter to over 100 environmental organizations. The situation blew up.

A lack of communication between government agencies was epidemic. The Department of Transportation and FAA, aligned with Miami business interests and the DCPA, had proceeded to make plans without notification except for mandatory filings in the *Federal Register.* The Department of the Interior, responsible for maintaining Everglades Park, was not always up to date on the rapidly developing project. And, most important, the DCPA had carefully disguised its long-range plan by applying for the airport as nothing more than a training site.

As public awareness of the project grew the media, particularly Miami newspapers, began to look hard at the history of land purchases around the airport site. They discovered that a number of dummy corporations had been set up in 1957, and with the definitive study as to location being made public eight years later the possibility of purchases based on insider information reared its ugly head. Adding to increased concern about the project, large sinkholes began to appear in central Florida, an indication that the water table was being affected by all the earlier drainage.

A public hearing in February 1969 hardened opposition. Attended by over 200 people, DCPA representatives were either unprepared or overly vague when answering questions on overall development plans. It became apparent that the port authority had done practically no analysis as to the environmental impacts. The meeting further eroded trust in the authority, but when conservation activists began to publicly criticize they were dismissed as "butterfly chasers" and "yellow-bellied sapsuckers." [41]

In response, the Everglades Coalition was formed in April 1969 with 21 members opposed to the rapid pace of events. It survives to this day as a broad-based organization with over 50 members dedicated to restoration of the greater Everglades ecosystem from the Kissimmee Lakes to Florida Bay, but the question posed in 1969 was: how to create an exit strategy that the DCPA and Miami business community could live with?

Saving the Big Cypress

The next chapter in the battle to save the swamp from supersonic jets began with a 1970 agreement between the federal government, DCPA and the State of Florida to look for a new airport site where regional impacts and environmental effects would be fully and transparently considered.[42] Getting to the pact was a hard and tortuous road. Joe Browder had once been a television journalist, but quickly eschewed the role of Cassandra for that of Ares. He became the National Audubon Society's south Florida representative and set out to change the minds of Floridians standing quietly by as their natural resources were being methodically destroyed. And he knew exactly who should lead the effort.

ENTER MARJORY DOUGLAS

After Marjory Stoneman Douglas wrote a book titled *The Everglades: River of Grass*, she withdrew from public participation in environmental issues until the matter of the jetport arose. Recruited by Browder, at the age of 78, she began a thirty-year crusade and became the rallying point for saving the Big Cypress. With the presence of Douglas, Joe Browder felt he had a forceful woman with a potentially large megaphone. It turned out to be a stroke of genius because she gave a human voice to the cause and it was hard to criticize a woman of Douglas' known stature.

Franklin Adams recalls:

The Friends of the Everglades was founded by Marjory to help fight the Big Cypress jetport which would have been located only a few miles north of Everglades National Park. You could become a member and supporter of the Friends for the grand sum of $1. Most of us gave at least $5. But I recall reviewing the Collier County list and the amount given by each person. One of Naples most wealthy men had actually joined at the $1 level. I guess that was how he made his fortune and hung on to it.

I can remember conversations with Marjory Douglas. You know she was very outspoken and she had very strong feelings about certain things. I once said to her 'Marjory, sometimes what you say in your arguments makes people mad' And she replied 'Franklin, when you get to be my age you can damn well say anything you want to.'

Browder, with the approach of a bulldog, had been able to bring the Big Cypress issue to a heavy boil by enlisting the Miccosukee Tribe, hunters and fishermen, and others into an organized conservation movement. With Johnny Jones, Executive Director of the Florida Wildlife Federation, he engaged Nathaniel Reed, Gov. Claude Kirk's environmental advisor, to initiate a political campaign to give the Big Cypress some sort of protection.

Browder and the rest of us wanted to protect the Big Cypress but not as a national park. We knew there would be too much opposition to trying to do so. So there was a lot of discussion as to possibilities including having Florida acquire the Cypress since Florida School Boards already owned all the Section 16's in each township plus other lands but we were afraid the State of Florida was not interested or not willing to take on the issues.

Called by the mayor of Dade County a "white militant," Reed was the wealthy scion of the family that developed Hobe Sound. Tall and articulate, he had been instrumental in getting Gov. Kirk to soften his original support for the jetport and later managed to get Walter Hickel, Secretary of the Interior to spend a night in the swamp with Gov. Kirk and a well-stocked supply of sour mash bourbon. Hickel immediately grasped the magnitude of the issue and returned to Washington as a convert. But the main problem was at the Department of Transportation, which had already signaled approval of the jetport. Hickel's solution was to have his deputy, Russell Train (who would later become the first secretary of the Environmental Protection Agency) appoint a select committee to study how the hydrology of the jetport would affect Everglades National Park. Gov. Kirk supported the idea of the study because it would give him political cover to walk back his initial approval of the project.

Chosen to head the study was Dr. Luna Leopold, the son of author Aldo Leopold, founder of the Wilderness Society and author of *Sand County Almanac*. Selected as the on-site study coordinator was Arthur Marshall. He was the south Florida representative of the Bureau of Sport Fisheries and Wildlife for the Department of the Interior, and a friend of Adams:

Kathy my wife and I were very fond of Art. He became a treasured friend and mentor to me as he did to others from the beginning when Marjory Douglas introduced me to Art at the Governors Water Conference in Miami Beach. Until his untimely passing we enjoyed discussing ideas and strategies by telephone mostly. I could hardly type then and Mrs. Douglas did no typing, she wrote everything in longhand, so we talked mostly in the evenings after work. Art reminded me of my father G. B. Adams. There were the eyeglasses, the facial resemblance and the same rich voice.

As opposition grew, Miami real estate companies and businesses supporting the jetport reacted by buying a series of ads in newspapers and radio stations across the state complaining about federal intervention in Florida land use and management. But much of that fell on deaf ears because the bulk of opposition was from Florida organizations, and had little to do with federal overreach.

THE STUDIES

The Leopold study strongly suggested that the only way to manage large developments was to insulate government from powerful outside influences, by creating a set of rules agreed to by all parties at interest, easily understood and rigorously enforced. It urged the governor's office and state legislature to take steps to establish land use planning at multiple levels, making Florida an exemplar among the states.

A second independent study released by the National Academy of Sciences, and written by noted physicist Murray Gell-Mann, came to the same conclusion. Along with Reed in Gov. Kirk's office, Gell-Mann became a staunch and vocal critic of the jetport by flatly asserting that draining the land around the airport would create a hydrologic nightmare.

A third and competing study, financed by the Dade County Commission and supported by the Chamber of Commerce, responded that many of the problems perceived by environmentalists might be solved by either existing or yet to be discovered technology, but was dismissed as overly speculative.

Once the Leopold study was released, along with the Gell-Mann report a day later, Hickel had settled science. Taking his case to the Department of Transportation and relying heavily on the disastrous effect of polluted water in the park, he convinced Secretary Volpe to halt airport construction.

In a joint press release newly elected Florida Gov. Ruben Askew (R-FL) in Tallahassee was joined by Sen. Lawton Chiles (D-FL) in Washington who commented that "...the Big Cypress is jeopardized by the pressure from progress based on sometimes well-intended, but too often ill planned development. The fate of the broad, flat, very gently sloping watershed in southwest Florida hangs in precarious balance. The Big Cypress has the potential for becoming a textbook, or classic example, of ecological ruin if we don't save it." [43]

Ever the politician President Richard Nixon, not known for enthusiastic support of environmental issues, inserted himself by announcing his plan for acquisition of the Big Cypress. With cabinet secretaries aligned, and Chiles and

Henry "Scoop" Jackson (D-WA) nipping at his heels, in November 1971 Nixon proposed to purchase 547,000 acres of land around the jetport site to create something called the "Big Cypress National Freshwater Preserve." Part of the timing may have been because Jackson felt the jetport was a perfect example of why laws were needed to require a careful analysis of similar projects. He had introduced the National Environmental Policy Act in the Congress in 1968 and using that as a platform, planned to make an announcement in Miami that he would be a candidate for the presidency.

With Nixon on the record and bipartisan support, in April 1972 Gov. Askew appeared before the U. S. Senate Subcommittee on Parks and Recreation to seek help from the federal government in acquiring the Big Cypress based upon recreational opportunities in the area and, more importantly, to protect Everglades National Park.

Adams clarified the difficulty of the moment:

The original focus was on water; hence the original name was the Big Cypress National Freshwater Reserve. The issue was how to protect water that flowed into Everglades National Park and Ten Thousand Islands. Eventually a compromise was reached after several years of disagreement and fighting and the Big Cypress would be a new breed of federal cat, a Preserve. It and Big Thicket would be the first ones.

Askew may have been the last hope for the development community, but his support for federal purchase was unwavering. Opponents then shifted to a standing trope—a federal government land grab of private property—anathema to many Floridians. The exact number of landowners within the Big Cypress boundary was uncertain, but what was known was that less than 100 people lived there on a permanent basis, and many lots were registered to out-of-state addresses.

ACSC

At the same time, the state was preparing to designate a section of Collier County as an Area of Critical State Concern (ACSC). Bringing the ACSC from concept to reality was, as with many things in Florida, not easy.

The ACSC program was part of the Florida Environmental Land and Water Management Act of 1972, the same bill that created the five water management districts. It was "...intended to protect resources and public facilities of major statewide significance, within the designated geographic areas, from uncontrolled development that would cause substantial deterioration of such resources."[44] It set out a series of rules, one of which was that the county's land development code had to provide that all permitting in the ACSC would have to be submitted for approval by the state.

A hearing held in Everglades City on September 5, 1973 drew over 500 angry people. According to a newspaper report, one incensed landowner stood up: "How would you like to live in a police state? We will be [living in one] with these proposed regulations. They would depreciate land values, tell you how you can use your land, or rather how you can't use it, and they're not going to give us one red cent." [45]

That brought a sharp retort from Marjory Douglas: "There must be progress, certainly. But we must ask ourselves what kind of progress we want, and what price we want to pay for it. If we want to destroy everything beautiful in our world, and contaminate the air we breathe, and the water we drink, then we are in trouble." [46]

The idea of a "police state" took hold and permeated the rhetoric from those opposed, although attorneys for the development interests and Collier companies were a bit more restrained. Two more hearings were scheduled for the next two days: one in Immokalee and the other at Naples Middle School. After the hearings hundreds of comments followed as written suggestions. The Division of State Planning issued its recommendation and scheduled a final hearing for November 13th at Naples High School. The meeting lasted for over 15 hours and once again all hell broke loose, but as a way out for the politicians, environmental groups offered to put the issue to a vote of the citizens in February, 1974 coinciding with the City of Naples election.

With that, major landowners (being the two Collier companies) convinced Rep. Lorenzo Walker of Collier

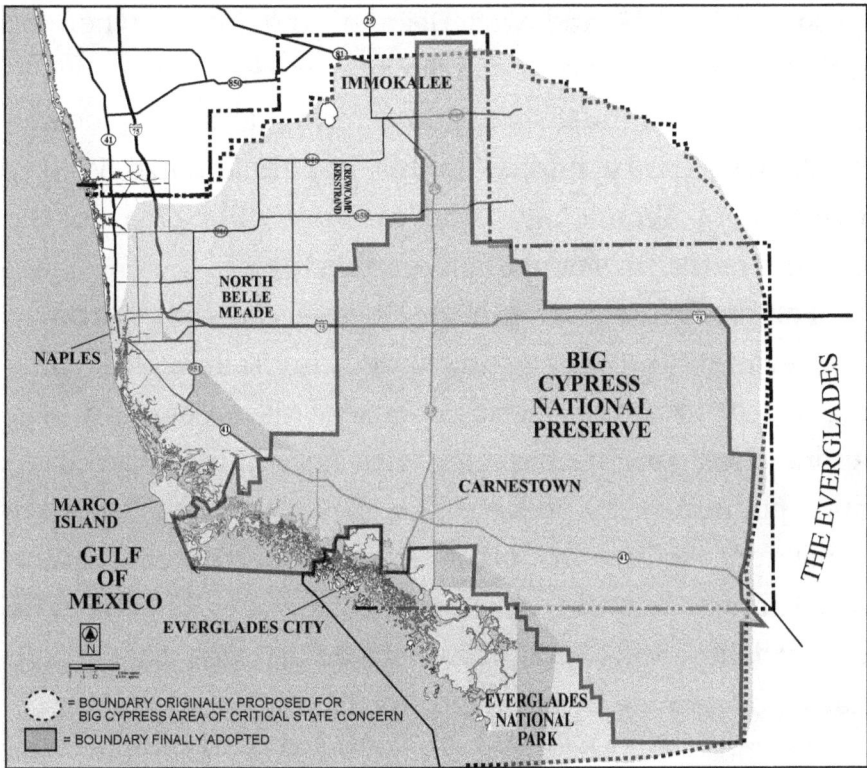

ACSC and Big Cypress Preserve original boundaries.
Map created by John G. Beriault.

County to introduce a bill to remove 80,000 acres from the proposed ACSC, all in what was called The Boot, otherwise known as the Okaloacoochee Slough, with headwaters all the way up into Hendry County, as shown on the map above.

Walker was well known in local politics. Starting in the real estate business he was elected to the Collier County Commission in 1950 and to the State House of Representatives from 1956-1974. He served as speaker from 1967-1968 and was Dean of the House when he retired from public office in November 1974. He managed to get a state-funded vocational technical school located in Collier County named in his honor: Lorenzo Walker Institute of Technology. And he was willing to do the bidding of the powerful Collier family.

For environmental groups, it was the first Battle of Roncevaux all over again. Based in Tallahassee, they organized into the Florida Conservation Coalition and approached pending hearings with near military precision and planning to present the best message to state legislators. Polling in Collier County was the centerpiece of their presentation where the vote was 4,334 for state stewardship and 1,522 against—a message that could hardly be ignored by elected officials.

To add to the cacophony of the moment the National Park Service announced it had problems with grandfathered ownership in the Big Cypress. With over 420 seasonal camps it was concerned that swamp buggies used for hunting would destroy the pristine wilderness. The Miccosukee and Seminole Tribes weighed in asserting their rights to traditional uses of the land which their ancestors had occupied for centuries. The Tribes had been instrumental in fighting the jetport and were regarded as important members of the group.

The only way out was to create consensus around a set of land use regulations, something never been done before in State of Florida. The issue was eventually muted, but not completely resolved, by Florida Wildlife Federation, a long-time supporter of a preserve entering the picture. The state chapter brought in the national organization's support with its large membership representing sportsmen and having enough political clout to bring about a satisfactory compromise.

But in an act well known in the halls of the Florida legislature two other bills were filed to revoke state control of the surrounding buffer zone and allow development along the edges of the new preserve. In a classic case of rope-a-dope, hearings on the Big Cypress Act and boundary changes were scheduled for the same hour on the same day. Hearings for Rep. Walker's bill HB2494 and a companion bill SB124 in the Senate, were scheduled on top of one another with the House Environmental Protection Committee at 8:15 a.m. and the Senate Natural Resources Committee at 8:00 or 8:30 a.m. A frustrated Askew stepped in and insisted the legislature pull the boundary shifting bill to a later hearing date. That never happened and both sides showed up in force. A family rancher named Joe Hilliard from the Big Cypress set out the farmers' argument:

> "My grandaddy came to this area in 1906 and we've been farming it ever since. We hate condominiums and developments; the farmer is the only true individualist still left in the country and y'all are really giving him a run for his money. The farmers were the first ecologists

in America and don't want to see development going on in their farming areas. Please don't force us to sell our farmlands. In conservation area three, hunters take hordes of dune buggies and race through the area with their hunting dogs, running deer down until they are just half-dead, jumping out of the buggy and slitting their throats or just walking up to the deer and shooting them in the head. None of this business goes on in my ranch." [47]

While speaking from the heart, Hilliard's remarks also broached the subject of how rules drafted by the Department of Pollution Control (DPC) might take the existing agriculture exemption out of its current status. At issue was Chapter 380, which allowed agriculture to continue provided the land was not planned or zoned for development.

In response a developer from Naples, Phillip Smithers, speaking for the Collier County Audubon Society took the other side:

"We haven't heard the real reason these people want the land to be removed from the buffer zone. All these ranchers and farmers are exempt so all their arguments are baloney. This is practically a private bill by a few landowners while the impact of the bill affects the entire county. All the designation does is to allow the surface waters to run their natural course, so it is really a zoning law and while it probably increases development costs those costs can be passed along to the buyer. Another reason they want their land removed could be for sale to Florida Power & Light for oil wildcatting operations in South and Central Florida."[48]

The original Senate bill sought to remove 285,000 acres but was amended to 88,000 acres and passed the committee 6-3.

Over on the House side it was a similar scene featuring opposing views. However, the first speaker at the committee hearing was with the Bureau of Land Planning, and his agency was against any removal of acreage from what was termed a "natural system."

In response, representing agriculture, Curt Kiser, brought up the spectre of property rights, as paraphrased below:

"I make my living in this area called the buffer zone, and [am speaking] on behalf of the entire 58,000 member Florida Farm Bureau Federation. Regulation of areas contiguous to the Big Cypress Swamp proper, i.e. the buffer zone, is an unnecessary erosion of basic property rights and would constitute a taking without due process and just compensation." [49]

A member of the DPC staff confirmed that fertilizers and pesticides would still be permitted in the farmlands of the ACSC, and with that the committee voted 12-4 to kill Lorenzo Walker's bill.

Franklin Adams was overjoyed. He sent a May 20th telegram to the chair of the House committee:

"Due to time limitation for testimony, I did not have the opportunity to present my testimony. For the record, I would like to thank the committee for their votes in opposition to Representative Walker's amended bill to delete the Okaloacoochee Slough from the Area of Critical State Concern." [50]

Subsequently, Representative Walker made the decision not to run for re-election. The Big Cypress designation remained intact, but there would other attempts in the future to modify the boundaries and to change land use regulations on agricultural lands. Many of them. That's just the way it is.

MAKING SAUSAGE

In May 1973, despite the multiplicity of objections and unanswered questions the Florida House and Senate passed the Big Cypress Conservation Act authorizing $40 million of state money to begin purchase. Then, it was up to the Congress to step in.

The real story of how it happened is best told by Johnny Jones:

> "I went to Washington, I think in the spring of 1973, to testify before the Senate Interior Subcommittee on Lands. Sen. Allen Bible, from Nevada, was the chairman of the committee. When we went before Sen. Bible's committee, I felt hostility. After the hearing, I said to Tom Kimball (Executive Director of the National Wildlife Federation) 'Sen. Bible is against us for some reason.' I asked Tom if he knew him, and if he could get us in to see him. Tom knew him quite well and got us an appointment that afternoon. When we got into Senator Bible's office, I asked him 'what is it you don't like about the bill?' He scowled at me, 'you people in Florida just got the Everglades National Park bought with federal money, and now you're back up here wanting more. Florida hasn't put any money on the table.' I asked him, 'How much money do you want from Florida?' He answered, '40%,' which amounted to about $40 million. 'If I can get Florida to put $40 million will you let the bill out of committee?' I asked. Senator Bible agreed.

"The Florida legislature was in session, so I went back to Tallahassee. I went straight to Gov. Ruben Askew's office. I told him that we're not going to get the Big Cypress approved by Congress unless we put up $40 million. We had just approved the Environmentally Endangered Lands bonding program in November 1972, so we had $240 million available, but the enabling legislation had not yet become effective, so we needed to pass a bill to get the money appropriated. Gov. Askew sent me to Sen. Bob Graham's office, where his staff chairman, Al Galbraith, Bernie Litz and I wrote a measure that would appropriate the $40 million. In the House, Representative Richard Pettigrew also had a bill that would put up $40 million if the federal government agreed to purchase of the entire Big Cypress. Graham's bill brought the first $40 million regardless of what the feds did. It passed the Senate and when it was sent to the house, Representative Pettigrew adopted Graham's version of the bill." [51]

A lot of the work was done by Johnny Jones. Johnny was one of those guys that could really talk to the politicians in Tallahassee and that was the ability you got have if you're going to get anything done.

With $40 million from the state and support from both Florida senators, the expectation was for quick passage of the appropriation. But that didn't happen. Once again in Jones's own words:

> "When the measure was passed into law, we notified Sen. Bible of Florida's commitment to the purchase of Big Cypress. He still refused to let the bill out of committee. Senator Henry "Scoop" Jackson, of Washington State, was chairman of the full Interior Committee. Tom Kimball went to Jackson and told him what Bible had said. Senator Jackson pulled the deal out of Bible's committee, and signed on as a sponsor. He and Sen. Chiles held hearings in Miami, and Jackson brought the bill to the floor of the Senate where it was approved." [52]

The bill appropriated up to $150 million and was sent off for presidential signature. Richard Nixon had resigned and on October 11, 1974 President Gerald Ford signed the bill creating the 583,000 acre Big Cypress National Preserve (BCNP), one of the first two preserves in the nation. It would "assure preservation, conservation, and protection of the natural, scenic, hydrologic, floral and faunal, and recreational values of the Big Cypress watershed in the state of Florida." [53]

CONTROVERSY NEVER ENDS

While the flap over the jetport was settled, Management of the preserve was not. Franklin Adams described the conundrum facing the Park Service:

> *The Park Service did not want to manage this new thing known as a Preserve, since it was not a National Park. They were given the management anyway. Problem with this compromise was, the National Park Service had no previous experience managing this new entity, it was not a park, a monument etc. It was something new. And there was a lot of controversy.*

Not everyone was excited by the prospect of government ownership and control.

"To Big Joe and many of the landowners and sportsmen along the trail the legal row that had ended the airport project and set the ball rolling for government purchase amounted to a disaster. Joe would rail to sympathetic ears against the huge federal land grab that was in the works. He and many others had probably hoped that the airport project would succeed. Essentially a scheme that would shoot land values over the moon by bringing a new Miami International Airport to their front doors, many business owners, speculators, and destitute folks who lived along the swampy corridor might suddenly be found on the good end of the stick." [54]

Jones was well aware of the dissonance:

"The Big Cypress acquisition was not a particularly popular concept among many of the residents of South Florida. Many people were still smarting from the loss of fishing and hunting opportunities that occurred when the Everglades National Park was created in the late 1940s. Many had moved their hunting camps from what is now the Park to the Cypress and now they feared they would be forced out. Many of these landowners built their camps with the intention to eventually retire to the area to live full-time." [55]

The other groups also smarting were the Miccosukee and Seminole Tribes. They had occupied the land for generations and were concerned that federal managers out of Washington, D.C. failed to understand how important parts of the land were for their traditional and ritual uses despite the fact that the act gave the Tribes rights to continue to hunt, trap and use the preserve for their own benefit, to continue to provide any existing tourist services within the preserve, and first right of refusal to provide visitor services. Tourist services had been one way for the tribes to earn a meager living, and legislators felt they had to make some minor accommodation to inhabitants whose ancestors had lived in the Big Cypress for generations.

These were small concessions given the fact that the tribes over time had claimed rights to over 30 million acres of land in Florida. This had been reduced to 4 million acres by the Treaty of Moultrie Creek aftere the First Seminole War, but the Miccosukee and Seminoles always had difficulty proving to the United States court system, accustomed to a paper trail of written documents, that they actually had deliverable title to the land. Property rights of the Indian nations had always been dealt with at the point of a bayonet.

THE POLITICS OF WILDERNESS

The Big Cypress bill affirmed preexisting private property rights to oil and gas extraction in perpetuity, and allowed limited grazing and water use, with the following proviso: "The owner of an improved property on the date of its acquisition by the Secretary may, as a condition of such acquisition, retain for himself and his heirs and assigns a right to use and occupancy of the improved property for a definite term of not more than 25 years or, in lieu thereof, for a term ending at the death of the owner or the death of his spouse, whichever is later." [56]

Existing rights were pretty much settled, but not the definition of a single word. That word was "wilderness." As described in the enabling Act of 1964, the definition was lyrical: "A wilderness, in contrast with those areas where man and his own works dominate the landscape, is hereby recognized as an area where the earth and its community of life are untrammeled by man, where man himself is a visitor who does not remain." [57]

One of the provisions of the act creating the BCNP was that the NPS was mandated to identify certain areas as "wilderness." This was an important distinction and one that carried a lot of baggage. The proposal, when released in 1979, concluded that no part of the preserve could be called "wilderness" because mineral rights were retained by private interests (mainly the Collier family). Besides, the area was crisscrossed with off-road vehicle trails tearing up the land. Faced with objections, the NPS promised to restudy the situation in 1984. Never happened.

> *No management plan or operator's manual or guide was ever given to them. So—for most of the history of the preserve (not a park) the NPS has tried to manage Big Cypress as a park, not a preserve where traditional uses are allowed such as ownership of private property, hunting, off road vehicles, oil exploration etc. This resulted in litigation by several environmental groups over the years.*

John Jones, who obtained the original $40 million for the state's share of the purchase, had his own opinion:

> "One of my greatest regrets is that I did not follow the Big Cypress issue through to its conclusion. I believe if I had remained active in the public debate that continued, I might have been able to keep alive in the issue of traditional uses. I am still convinced that the traditional swamp buggies, which were built lightweight, with limited horsepower and wide tires, should be allowed. The Big Cypress is a watershed that provides water to the park. It is not, and never was intended to be an extension of Everglades National Park. It was to be a buffer and recreational uses were to be maximized. Sen. Chiles was particularly adamant about keeping the Big Cypress open to hunting, fishing and camping. I am outraged that the bureaucrats are attempting to subvert the intent of the original law to fit their own intents and purposes." [58]

Adams chimed in:

I built my first swamp buggy in my parents' backyard when I was in high school. Back then most buggies were of relatively small size and weight. Built primarily from

Model-A Ford or Jeep running gear. Mine weighed 1430 lbs. What became known as those buggy trails in the Big Cypress were the old logging and farming roads whose impact had already mostly occurred. Buggies were necessary if you were going to spend time in the backcountry to haul your gear, build a camp etc. Swamp buggies today are of many kinds. More people today are using manufactured side by sides and 4-wheelers rather than homemade swamp buggies. They are necessary equipment used by Florida Fish & Wildlife Law Enforcement, National Preserve Law Enforcement rangers, biologists, researchers, fire crews and inspected, permitted and licensed members of the public as permitted by the Big Cypress legislation. Yes those trails and ruts look like hell from the air or on the ground. But some visual and surface impacts are to be expected from this necessary and authorized use. Some environmental groups have greatly exaggerated the impacts and litigated against the National Park Service (NPS) over the years.

Adams and Jones both had a point. Sec. 5 of the Big Cypress Act provided that:

"...the Secretary shall permit hunting, fishing, and trapping on lands and waters under his jurisdiction within the preserve in accordance with the applicable laws of the United States and the state of Florida, except that he may designate zones where and periods when no hunting, fishing, trapping, or entry may be permitted for reasons of public safety, administration, floral and formal protection and management, or public use and enjoyment." [59]

Adams makes a further point:

NPS has tried to address these concerns developing an off-road system of primary and secondary trails which only permits trails to exist in approximately one percent of the entire Preserve acreage. A large part of the Preserve has been totally closed for many years to any vehicular access. Examples being inside the Loop, Deep Lake, and Airplane Prairie, the Addition Lands and now Windmill Prairie and the lands in the Mullet Slough area are proposed wilderness.

The controversy over what is "wilderness" continues to the present day.

LONG TERM IMPACTS

The Big Cypress jetport controversy had a tectonic effect on the nation and the State of Florida. The absence of formal land use planning had allowed special interests to press their case with little regard to the effects on the larger ecosystem and the broader public interest. The airport controversy represented a tipping point between the prior world of unrestrained development of industry and agriculture and a new world in which environmental factors had to be considered, not only for negative impacts but also for positive benefits accruing to the larger population.

Implicit in the Leopold report were two important ideas: first, that independent scientists should be given the responsibility to propose standards of air and water quality to preserve and restore natural resources insofar as possible and second, that land use planning should be codified and coordinated at the various levels of government.

Those recommendations gained purchase in Tallahassee and the state legislature went to work. The Florida Water Resources Act was passed in 1972, creating five water management districts throughout the state. It was a brilliant move because each venue was based on watersheds rather than traditional geopolitical boundaries. The South Florida Water Management District was the first and largest, covering 18,000 sq. mi, or 30% of the land mass of the state. Also passed in 1972 was the Florida Land and Water Conservation Act (LCA), created to purchase environmentally sensitive lands within the state. It would be funded by a tax on the transfer of real estate titles and provide an ongoing supply of funds for land acquisition.

A powerful new law came out of Washington. In December 1969 the Senate passed Sen. Jackson's National Environmental Policy Act (NEPA), creating the Council on Environmental Quality. It set out a system whereby any development in critical lands would have to be analyzed with an environmental impact statement.

The Clean Water Act amended the Federal Water Pollution Control Act of 1948, giving EPA broad discretion on managing water quality and expanding U. S. Army Corps of Engineers jurisdiction over "waters of the United States." The Act did not define "waters" but left it to discretion of EPA and the Department of the Army to regulate. [60] Broadly interpreted, it meant that seasonal ponds, lakes, bogs, mud holes and swamps fell under the federal umbrella. The law allowed the Corps to deny permits based upon potential downstream damage to water bodies, a higher hurdle than the prior law. The underlying issue was that fresh water being stored in the interior and released gradually through rivers and creeks allowed wetlands to go through annual seasonal cycles. The diffused groundwater once it reached coastal estuaries had nurtured habitats established over centuries where stationary filter feeders like clams and oysters, as well as cleansing sea grasses, had been established and thrived for decades, and needed to be carefully managed.

Adding to the momentum of the era, the Florida legislature passed a series of bills in the 1980s to bring land management planning into a formal rubric starting at the local level and moving through regional planning councils up to the state's new Department of Community Affairs. It marked the beginning of a period where a holistic view of environmental issues was adopted and transformed into legislative reality. Gov. Bob Graham became a leader and advocate for environmental restoration but it had taken a little doing.

I remember when Gov. Bob Graham seemed to forget about conservation issues and the Glades. Art Marshall and Johnny Jones could not seem to get a meeting. Then a reporter named Robert Boyle came down to Florida to write an article for Sports Illustrated magazine on the politics of the Everglades and the need for repairing them. Art and Johnny met with Boyle. They criticized the governor, something to the effect that he had become inaccessible on Everglades issues. No sooner had the issue of the magazine hit the newsstands than the governor's office immediately called to set up a meeting with Graham. How fortuitous. That issue of Sports Illustrated was the very first "swimsuit issue" and received wide publicity in the media and in homes and barbershops. It reached many who had been unaware of the Everglades issues, Big Sugar and politics. Art invited me to accompany him and Johnny to be with the governor, however I could not. Have always wished that I could have been there as I consider it one of the turning points in the right direction for the

Everglades. From then on, Bob Graham was attentive to whatever Art, Johnny and Marjory Douglas had to say.

The spate of new laws opened opportunities to put vast areas of land into conservation for public use. It was not an easy transition because the mechanisms of state government, and much of the staff, had been attuned to fostering economic development and moving land into public ownership meant lower *ad valorem* tax receipts. In addition, many long-time elected government officials and appointed staff harbored a suspicion about the new generation of environmental advocates with their reliance on science to buttress their arguments.

Adams felt Marshall was struggling with the political side of many decisions.

There were times when Art was for lack of better terms down discouraged or depressed. Because Art was correct in his assessments and his recommendations he was quickly ostracized, ignored or excluded from the bureaucratic circles and discussions. They somehow felt threatened by this "outsider." Especially the agency "scientists." Art's message was pure and simple apart from politics.

11-MILE ROAD

Many in the conservation movement knew that in the effort to preserve natural resources there were no permanent victories, only temporary truces save buying land into public ownership. The story of the 11-mile road into the Big Cypress was a classic case on point. It is a small example of the continuing need for citizen involvement in the government agencies and an illustration of how money plays in Florida politics.

While the state was buying up land in the Big Cypress, oil drilling and exploration by the Collier interests continued. The Raccoon Point well field, just north of the jetport training site, had been accessed by an 11-mile road from the Tamiami Trail to five wells being pumped by Exxon. The road, following old swamp buggy trails, was objected to by the Florida Wildlife Federation. Approved in 1976, it was designed to be temporary, but could become permanent if more oil was discovered. The company had plans to drill another 25 wells, and Adams was on it:.

The 11-mile road had been permitted and constructed soon after with the agreement of the National Park Service since it was in the Big Cypress Preserve. The Preserve at that time didn't have a superintendent so was under the supervision of the Everglades Park. Then, six years later, the National Park Service decided that it wanted Exxon to remove the entire 11-mile road and build a new one south from Alligator Alley down to Raccoon Point.

Two problems emerged. First, Alligator Alley was scheduled to be upgraded to I-75 and would require an interchange to access a road that led only to oil fields. Second, the proposal drew immediate and strong criticism from the head of the Florida Fresh Water Fish and Game Commission, Robert Brantly:

"Perhaps fewer than 20 total panthers remain, making the species one of the most endangered in the world. Our margin for error in exploiting the habitat is obviously extremely narrow. It is, therefore, incumbent upon the Commission, as the State agency responsible for managing Florida's terrestrial wildlife, to take all necessary measures to ensure the continued survival of that species.

"The access road for which the Exxon Company has requested a permit to construct from Alligator Alley southward toward the Eleven Mile Road is a dramatic example of the type of access that will adversely impact the Florida panther. If that road is constructed, it will bisect on the last three remaining panther population centers and provide vehicular access into a specific area that currently is not only inaccessible by road, but it is also the Raccoon Point area, it is also a critical center of activity for at least four of those panthers. The four panthers there represent 20 per cent or more of the known population." [61]

In 1981, I was appointed by Gov. Bob Graham to the Big Cypress Swamp Advisory Committee, the one started by Gov. Askew, as representative of environmental organizations. My first committee meeting and field trip on the road lasted three days, and I discovered that it was the most controversial issue that the BCSAC had dealt with according to the other members. The BCSAC was very effective because its recommendations went right to the governor and Cabinet for their consideration, not to the agencies involved.

Brantly's objections were supported by Audubon, but both relented when Exxon offered a $30,000 grant to study the panthers' range and habitat. According to a newspaper report: "Exxon's offer was not without precedent. Brantly said two other companies with oil operations in the Big Cypress—Hughes Oil Company and National Resources Development—had each given $30,000 to the game commission for panther studies." [62] The road seemed on its way to approval but one organization, of which Franklin Adams was a large part, joined by the Sierra Club, was still opposed.

The Florida Wildlife Federation which had strongly opposed the construction of the original 11-Mile Road was contemplating litigation. The Big Cypress Swamp Advisory Committee did a field inspection of the proposed new road route by helicopter since there were no existing swamp buggy trails to travel on in some of the proposed new route requested. I recommended to the other committee members that they make a recommendation opposing the new Exxon road that the park service was requesting. The committee's final recommendation to the governor and cabinet was no new road coming down from the Alligator Alley to the Raccoon Point oil field location and it was not permitted.

To substantiate the point that it is "never over 'til it's over," in July 2014 the Hughes Oil Company and Collier Resources Company terminated their lease agreement, leaving out the Collier Hogan 20-3H well southwest of Lake Trafford, after the Department of Environmental Protection threatened to pull the permit. The company also decided to not drill near populated areas in Golden Gate Estates. Fast forward eight years and problems related to oil discovery under the Big Cypress continue with a controversy over seismic testing, as thumper trucks rove through the preserve, scattering wildlife and tearing up vegetation and wetlands with little repair to the damage done.

Home of the Ghost

We will now turn to the stories of how, after the bruising battle to save the Big Cypress, hundreds of thousands of additional acres were added to the initial 538,000. To do this we begin with the tale of the Fakahatchee Strand, host to the largest collection of native orchids in North America.

The Fakahatchee was ecologically and geologically unique, a deep depression draining the Camp Keais Slough and part of the Okaloacoochee Slough into Rookery Bay and the Ten Thousand Islands. It was a twenty-five-mile long wetland ideal for growing of myriad bromeliads and orchids.

In 1922 when Henry Ford, a winter resident of Fort Myers Florida, visited the Fakahatchee and he was taken by its virgin wild beauty and wanted to purchase and donate it to the State of Florida. The Lee Tidewater Cypress Company gave him an option for $2,250,000, but the state refused to take him up on the offer. It had enough "swamp land" and this would remove it from the tax rolls.

The later history of the Fakahatchee was written by the cypress logging industry. As demand increased with World War II, towns sprouted up along SR 29 to store equipment and provide employee housing. They also become transfer points where tram roads met the Atlantic Coast Line's main line to deliver timber north. When the strand was finally logged out, there was little traffic for the railroad so it tore up the tracks from Sunniland to Everglades City in 1957 and put its locomotives up for sale. The Jerome sawmill was closed but construction of the rail line, with connections to the logging industry's tram roads, had dramatically altered the hydrology of the area. Once abandoned by logging companies, the Fakahatchee was left populated by a few loners who desired to live far from civilization and did not welcome the presence of strangers. Adams knew it well:

While hiking in the Fakahatchee down a tram one day I saw a tar paper house with a man with a shotgun who glared at me so I stopped and backed up and left. Occasionally there were truck and buggies taken and if you were on the road you waved and were respectful and if you got stuck you might be able to ask for help. You did not ask for names or pry.

But that isolation did not last, because the idea of drying out swampland, widespread throughout Florida ever since Napoleon Bonaparte Broward's "Empire of the Everglades,"

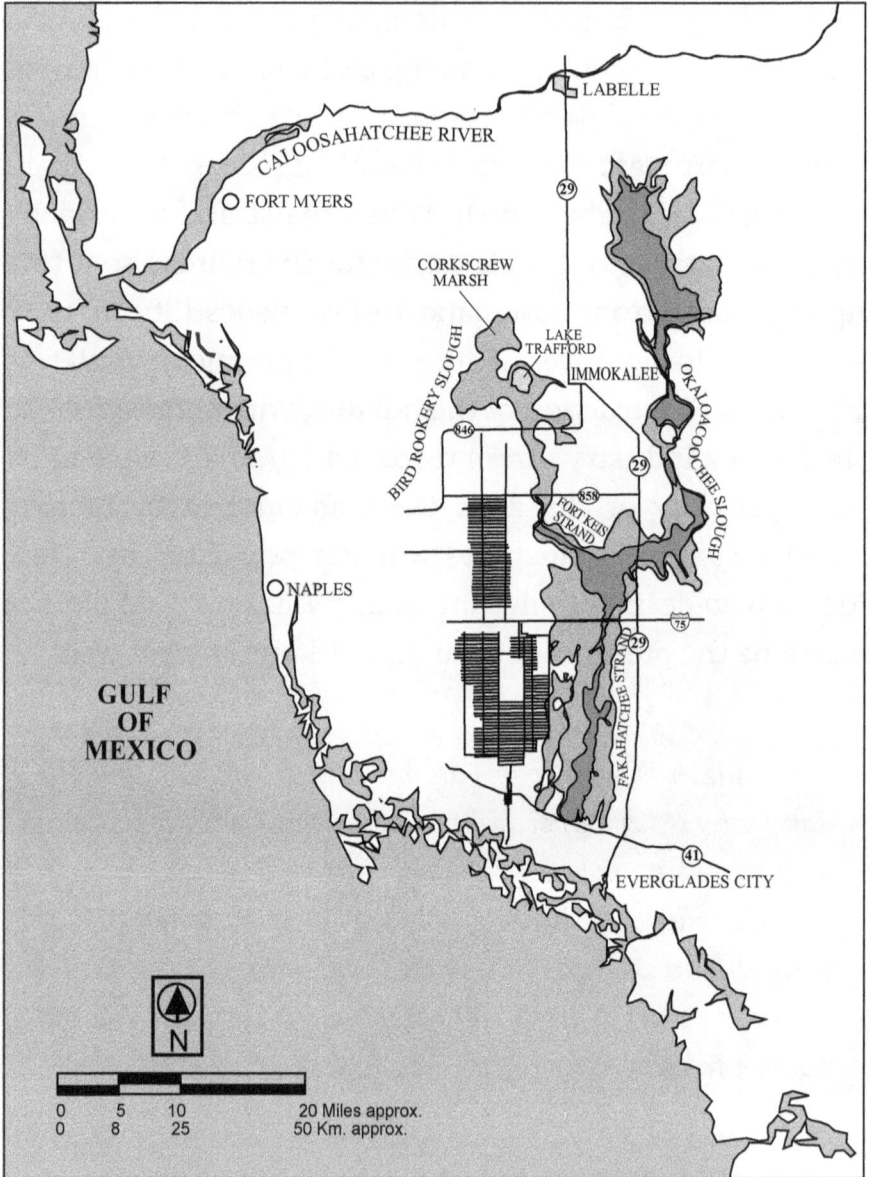

Fakahatchee Strand and Okaloacoochee Slough.
Map created by John G. Beriault.

was not lost on two speculators heavily invested in Lee County who saw another opportunity to the south.

ROSEN BROTHERS

The Rosen brothers had risen from modest beginnings in Baltimore as street vendors to build a mini conglomerate. Their prize product was Formula #9, a shampoo favored by women and promoted heavily through the new medium of television. But they had bigger ideas beyond cosmetics.

Leonard Rosen, with a history of health problems, was a regular visitor to south Florida. Loud, profane and aggressive as a promoter, he saw ads for lots at "$10 down and $10 a month," an enticing sales pitch which he could immediately embrace. Convincing his brother Jack, a bookish and professorial type, to invest they formed the Gulf American Land Corporation (GALC) and set their sights on a mangrove forest sitting a few feet above mean sea level, and good for little else other than as a nursery for fish and crabs. Nearby Fort Myers was little more than a fishing village and a spot where a few northerners, including Thomas Edison, came to escape the winter blasts.

In 1957, with high-interest loans backed by the Pritzker family of Chicago, the Rosens purchased 103 sq. mi of mangroves and low-lying land in Lee County for $678,000. It was owned by Dr. Franklin Miles, of Miles Laboratories—whose One-A-Day vitamins were a best seller at the time. They called it Cape Coral. In 1960, they added to their holdings buying the adjacent 16,000 acre Matlacha Ranch from sportsman and racehorse breeder Ogden Phipps.

Leonard Rosen knew he needed someone experienced in Florida land development who could work the system and while visiting a spa at Punta Gorda struck up a conversation with Milt Mendelsohn, who was dredging up 2,000 acres and selling lots in a subdivision called Harbor Heights. Always eager for more business, Mendelsohn agreed to guide the effort.

The standard building practice at the time was dredge and fill. Used successfully by the Mackle brothers at Marco Island, the technique was simple. With bucket dredges or drag lines, bottom muck was scraped up creating a canal and deposited to build a mound. Once high enough, the mound's edges would be contained by concrete seawalls. The muck was then given time to settle and dry, compressed by rollers, and made ready for utilities, roads and houses. By 1965, GALC was the largest land development company in Florida.

ENTER MEL FINN

Efforts to save the swamp had begun in 1962 with formation of the Fakahatchee Strand Committee. It was promoted by two people, an orchid-loving lawyer from Miami named Mel Finn who recruited an organizational dynamo, Jane Parks, Conservation Chair of the powerful Florida Federation of Women's Clubs, an organization committed to saving land, most notably Paradise Key adjacent to Homestead which would be made into Royal Palm State Park in 1969 from land donated by Henry Flagler's railroad. [63]

Mel was a lawyer over in Miami and being a lover of orchids, he was determined to save the Fakahatchee. Despite heavy logging there were still some natural areas left and he visited those often and recruited me to take people in to see the beauty of the place. I would say that Mel was more than determined, he was really obsessed.

Finn was also founder of the Florida chapter of the Nature Conservancy and had identified 45 varieties of orchids while visiting the Fakahatchee. In a letter to Parks in 1964, he admitted:

"Jane, I am devoting all my spare time and often a lot of my client's time to the Fakahatchee. I feel tremendously encouraged, especially when someone like you matches, if not surpasses, my own devotion to this project. I do believe it is catching on, to say the least. It is my conviction that we will be successful in the Fakahatchee undertaking. It is just a question of time and an unrelenting effort on everybody's part." [64]

Parks' idea was to somehow buy the land. She and Finn began by attempting to raise private funds, expecting the price of a logged out swamp to be no more than $10 per acre, but by 1963 the price had increased to $100. Reason was a two lane toll road from Naples to Fort Lauderdale known as the Everglades Parkway, and known to locals as "death row," provided convenient access into the strand from both the west and east coast. Franklin concurred:

> *As I recall, the going price was indeed $10 per acre for a 640 acre section and that is what Mel and Jane and I had talked about and planned on if we were successful in getting the Fakahatchee acquired. The reason the price went to $100 is simple. That's what the Rosens offered the Turner Corporation—$100 per acre on paper. Agreement was when the Rosens would sell an acre, they would then pay Turner the $100, not upfront. And the Rosens were aware we were trying to acquire the Fakahatchee.*

At the time, most of the impetus for buying land in the Fakahatchee came from Miami. There was little enthusiasm from the west coast because conservation organizations there had put all their resources into saving coastal areas like Rookery Bay and the Ten Thousand Islands. Fundraising went slowly so Parks and Finn then shifted their focus and tried to convince the state to buy it, but that stalled.

The emphasis in Florida was all about development, so they shifted again and tried to get the federal government interested. To do that Parks' powerful little committee, along with the Nature Conservancy, approached Congressman Paul Rogers (D-FL) to have the Fakahatchee designated as a National Monument. Adams, representing the Izaak Walton League, chimed in:

The area of which I am concerned is the Fakahatchee Strand of Collier County. The hour is late and direct action must be taken to save this truly unique ecological area. It is certainly worth much more as one of nature's masterpieces than it is as just another tract of land to be exploited for the temporary monetary gain of a few individuals. I would therefore ask you to devote your full support to having Fakahatchee Strand preserve as a national monument. [65]

Rogers did everything he could. He appeared in Naples in January 1966 at a public meeting and introduced a bill in the House, but his proposal for an appropriation failed because the money was diverted to another Florida project: the Biscayne National Monument.

After failed efforts by Parks' group and Finn to get the state interested, and with federal funding gone, in February 1966 the Rosens purchased 63,000 acres from the Turner

Company. Every acre was in the Fakahatchee watershed. The price was $6,326,000.

The Fakahatchee was critical for the Rosens because to the west was a large area of slightly elevated land, the Picayune Strand, that would be marketed as Southern Golden Gate Estates, a 42,000 acre piece of their 112,000 acre holding from I-75 all the way down to US41. It had a singular purpose: to drain areas to the north where the Rosens were selling lots in the 70,000 acre northern Estates. It would be accomplished by building a series of canals all tied into a single outlet called the Faka-Union running through a new development called Port of the Islands at the south end of the property. The system would drain the northern Estates but with 130 miles of new canals collecting up to 400 million gallons per day during the rainy season, the runoff came loaded with doses of nutrients pouring directly into Fakahatchee Bay in the Ten Thousand Islands to Adams' dismay.

Prior to the Rosens turning the Faka-Union River into a ditch we used to go downstream and collect tasty oysters from Fakahatchee Bay, return home, and invite the neighbors over for raw or grilled oysters. That ended with all the nutrient runoff from the drainage canals into what was then called the South Blocks going downstream to pollute the bay.

The natural filtration of slow moving water was gone. Nutrients started killing sea grasses compromising the entire ecosystem and as the water table was lowered the hydrologic head became less resistant and salt water began to infiltrate ground water. As a result, the southern 42,000 acres, covered with cabbage palm, saw palmetto and seasonal wet marshes was only marginally habitable.

To sooth the rising tempers of sport fishermen about the future of water quality at Fakahatchee Bay, Rosen's representative, General Charles Jung, revealed a new development plan. Known as the Remuda Ranch, it would have "... camp sites, riding stables, a shooting range, picnic areas and nature trails." There would also be a hotel, marina with numerous docks. Then, he made a bold promise: "It will not be cut into lots. Because of the tremendous interest shown by sportsmen and conservationists in this tract, and as a result of GALC's outstanding success with River Ranch, it plans to leave a large portion of the tract in its natural state." [66]

His comforting statement was viewed with skepticism because closing documents told a different story. The documents were clear and unambiguous: "It is understood that that the mortgagor intends to subdivide the land encumbered hereby and to be able to do so in conformity with the real estate laws of Florida providing for releases conforming to that law." [67]

Despite mounting problems, the company went into full sales mode in 1966 offering 1,000 S & H Green Stamps to anyone who would visit the Gulf Coast to look at property. A coupon was appended to newspaper ads throughout the country offering the stamp giveaway and a no-obligation free air tour. The message was inviting:

> "Golden Gate visitors will tour Gulf American's second preplanned community, located just nine road miles northeast of Naples. They'll visit the luxurious country club with its championship nine hole golf course and resort motel. They'll walk through made to order Florida homes, including the revealing 'cutaway house' which demonstrates step-by-step quality construction here at Golden Gate where visitors will see America's men and machines literally changing the face of Florida." [68]

At the time, Florida land sales were regulated by the 1964 Installment Land Sales Act, overseen by a five-member board appointed by the governor. Three of the five were affiliated with Gulf American because the state legislature, with a go-go attitude toward development, had insisted that the board have three members from the real estate industry. Leonard Rosen had been a member but resigned when the state Senate called him to testify on the growing number of complaints about his company's sales practices. With that Rosen had jumped off his powerful perch, a break because Gov. Kirk was only able to appoint, but not remove, board members.

After years of complaints and bureaucratic inaction, in 1967 Kirk convinced the legislature to do away with the 1964 act and replace it to create something called the Florida Land Sales Board. He gained the ability to remove members as part of the bill, and appointed a completely new board. The sales practices of the Rosen brothers came under immediate and microscopic scrutiny. [69]

Frustrated and facing the likelihood of severe financial penalties, in 1968 Gulf American sold to a company from Philadelphia: General Acceptance Corporation which assumed ownership through its oddly named subsidiary GAC Properties. Despite the sale the Rosens did not do badly. They had sold thousands of lots in Golden Gate for over $100 million and the deal with GAC was stock-for-stock so they continued to have a financial presence in south Florida real estate.

Not much changed. GAC Properties continued to sell lots at $1,000 each using high pressure tactics. But environmental groups, feeding on success from the jetport controversy, were becoming more aggressive and litigious. In addition, a number of studies had been done about water quality in south Florida canals. One study by the National Park Service about water flowing into Everglades National Park from the Big Cypress, was being shopped to get the Secretary of the Interior to take another look because the central part of the shallow depression that drained the

Camp Keais Strand and Okaloacoochee Slough was a major feeder into the park.

With the interest in Washington picking up the issue was beginning to attract national attention and negative publicity, so the company decided to stop selling in the Remuda Ranch and offered owners to swap for property up in Cape Coral.

On April 30, 1970, I picked up Mel Finn in Miami and we drove over to Everglades City to meet Governor Claude Kirk's Conservation Aide, Nathaniel Reed. Our purpose was to show Nat Reed the Fakahatchee Strand. Our hope was that the State of Florida would purchase as much of the Fakahatchee Strand as possible.

Mel and I met Nat, Ney Landrum Director of the Florida Outdoor Recreation Department, and Joel Kuperberg from Naples, Jim Sayes and Ken Alvarez a recently hired naturalist with the Florida State Parks Department at the Rod & Gun Club in Everglades City in the evening. After visiting with the group we all went over to the Illinois Motel where Mel and I were staying. It was less expensive than the Rod & Gun Club. Mel gave a fine slide presentation on the Fakahatchee. The purpose of the presentation was to educate and to give the group an idea of what they could expect on their hike/wade into the strand. Everyone, especially Nat Reed, seemed enthusiastic about our early morning hike/wade into the swamp strand.

At 1:30 in the morning my sister Layne called to say that Mom had passed away just after midnight during which time I had been suddenly and mysteriously ill with uncontrollable shaking and chills. Mel was concerned and wanted to call the town emergency people but I declined and my episode disappeared soon after. So I returned to Miami to be with family in the morning. Mel took the group into what we called Long Lake in the central drainage of the Fakahatchee which was one of our favorite areas to visit. Sunday morning Mel called me to say everyone was impressed and thrilled and Nat Reed promised to push our efforts to save the Fakahatchee up in Tallahassee. It was a very productive swamp walk. A new beginning.

Reed, at the time Chairman of the Florida Pollution Control Agency, tells the story of his trip into the Fakahatchee while Adams was in Miami with his family:

"George Gardner, my newly appointed assistant, came with a machete and we were outfitted with a five-foot-long stick to persuade water snakes and the occasional moccasin to move out of our way. After our walk we began to return to the starting site and George had taken out his machete and swung against a vine, but it bounced off and cut his leg very deeply. I help apply the tourniquet. I said 'George, you are too big to carry. You're going to have to be very brave and we will move as quickly as we can to the road when we get you to a hospital.' We mushed our way back to the waiting point with a state trooper's car was waiting. I sent George back to the airport and the rest of us huddled together, overcome by the sights of the Fakahatchee. Suddenly, an obvious rental car drove up and paused next to us. Two delightful ladies in the mid-50s inquired where they were. I answered 'in the middle of the Fakahatchee Strand.' 'No, no,' snapped one of them, 'it's quite impossible. We have been paying monthly for land to retire on. We thought that was near the Gulf, certainly not within a very wet swamp! Our ranch, which we bought from the Gulf American Company is right around here.' I had the unpleasant assignment of informing her that the Rosens were facing both state and federal government legal actions as sellers of swampland all across Southwest Florida. They exclaimed: 'This is an outrage! How can Florida's government allow such larceny? We are going back to their sales office and attempt to cancel our sale contract and will never return again to this hideous swamp!'" [70]

OVERDREDGING COMPENSATION

In addition to angry buyers like the "delightful ladies," another of the inherited problems was the ongoing negotiation for General American's overdredging 170 acres beyond the bulkhead line and into state sovereign lands to build Cape Coral in Lee County. GAC felt the need to clean up the public relations problem. Ney Landrum in Tallahassee, the new State Parks Director, floated the idea that a donation of property might settle the issue and in October 1970 Internal Improvement Fund trustees were offered 20,000 acres of land in the Fakahatchee in lieu of a cash fine for overdredging by GAC's predecessor.

The penalty had been initially set at anywhere between $765,000 and $2 million, but the J.C. Turner Lumber Company, original owner of the land, had gone to court in 1962 to prove to the Collier County tax assessor the entire strand was worth no more than $10,000. Despite that being on the record, GAC properties argued that it was worth $20 million based upon their sales of undeveloped land in the Remuda Ranch. The difference could not be bridged, so the deal didn't make, but it represented the first step in a long process to bring the Fakahatchee into public ownership.

IN THE FAKAHATCHEE—MAY 16, 1970

I picked Mel Finn at his home in Miami at 6:00 am and we drove to Copeland Grade to spend the day in the Fakahatchee, a place we dearly loved. We left the grade and walked down the tram approximately 20 minutes and then we turned east into the strand. On the way we saw a lot of otter and deer sign. On reaching the central flow way of the strand we took a compass bearing and headed north. Our destination today was Guzmania Gulch and Long Lake, a lake that has never been dry or burned to our knowledge. Our plan was to hit a large pond by following the water flow north but evidently we didn't go far enough east before turning north. We had not visited this pond before which shows on an aerial photo from the 1940's. We had left the main tram at 8:50 am. At 10:10 we crossed the first interior tram where we saw a cottonmouth attempting to swallow a Banded water snake. We disturbed the moccasin so that it released the banded water but then it continued searching for its prey as we watched.

We continued north until we hit the second tram. This tram must be crossed at a particular spot to assure hitting Long Lake and the Guzmania area. I noticed that the water on the south side of the tram was flowing east. The reason for this being that there was previously an old bridge culvert on the tram during the logging days and this seems to have been the very center of the main flowage way in Fakahatchee. The bridge and culvert are long gone but the water naturally funnels into this area of the tram and continues its slow natural drainage southwest. So in order to find the gap in the tram we walked (stumbled) up the direction of the flow west until we arrived at the crossing through where the water was deep and cold. The bottom was a sandy clear dotted with many small fish. I paused there for a moment to drink in some of that pure cool water and the beauty of the area.

There is a large oak just south of the gap, and a tall Royal palm just west of the gap. Leaving the crossing you must take a north to north-easterly compass course to hit Long Lake and Guzmania. Mel and I went slightly too far northwest and missed Guzmania and came up on the southwest corner of Long Lake which had grown up into a dense area of cut grass. Most of the lakes in the central strand are clear and open, surrounded by pond apple on the north ends but growth is heavy on the south ends with zizaniopsis.

Finding Long Lake it was a simple matter to correct ourselves and enter the Gulch where the water is cool and clear year round due to deeper water and shade. We spent a couple hours just wandering and enjoying this beautiful botanical treasure which is only a small part of Fakahatchee. We photographed the Guzmania in bloom although with the deep shade the lighting was very misleading.

Walking back out I led the way as Mel had walked up on the second snake of the day which was a banded water, not a cottonmouth this time. We walked out to the tram in 55 minutes which Mel recalled was the shortest time we had made the return trip. Buttonbush, Virginia willow, Caesar weed, Epidendrum anceps, and Polyrrhiza lindenii were all observed in bloom. We jumped four armadillos on the tram as we were walking out. These were the first armadillos I had ever seen in Fakahatchee or Collier County that I can recall.

There were a couple of dudes with a jeep buggy and I use the term buggy loosely tearing up the tram. They were hauling a flat trailer to their camp back by a small prairie on the left as you walk in. One fellow who owned the camp was Gary Keller or Kellum. Mel and I kidded them about trying to develop a camp, instead of just enjoying the woods. We talked to them about conservation and they of course informed us that they wouldn't destroy anything unless they could eat it or sell it.

CLOSING THE DEAL

Negotiations continued at a measured pace until 1972 when the Florida legislature created the Land Conservation

Act. Florida voters then approved issuance of $240 million in bonds for the Environmentally Endangered Lands (EEL) program, and money became available to buy land resurrecting old concerns about Section 380 of the Florida Statutes.[71] GAC felt that designation of the Fakahatchee, as part of the state's new Big Cypress ACSC coming out of the jetport settlement, would choke development because it came with a set of rules controlling the application of chemicals and fertilizers, nonpoint source nutrient concentrations, discharge of industrial waste, and restrictions as to construction or installation of septic tanks and associated drain fields.

GAC was still selling property in the northern Estates and in an attempt to mitigate environmental objections the company announced it would establish a new institution called the Fakahatchee Environmental Studies Center. Located at a facility at Port of the Islands and run by Cedar Crest College of Allentown Pennsylvania, it would open in late 1972 with a curriculum designed to create a better understanding of subtropical marine environments. The school did open briefly but soon after shut its doors.

In another move to dampen growing criticism, in January 1973 GAC announced plans to build 7,000 homes in a grasslands area called the Dan House Prairie at the Big Bend on the Trail. The 4,000 acre development would lie at the edge of the Remuda Ranch and involve a series of finger canals with mechanized gates to restore sheet flow that would mimic the seasonal pattern of Florida's wet and dry seasons.

It was part of a larger plan where well to the north GAC planned to elevate the main weir at the east-west Golden Gate Canal from 2 feet to 3½ feet to allow "sidewise diversion of the waterfall." [72] The goal was to raise the output level into the canal, which drained water from as far away as Corkscrew Swamp Sanctuary, then spread the water out and, when added to a mixing pond, replicate the original sheet flow of the system.

The whole project depended upon the county relocating the salinity line and allowing GAC to build a 250-acre lake just north of the Trail. The line had been established in 1964 and moving it would allow water to flow into a new pond along the south side of the Trail. From there it would spread naturally into the coastal mangrove forests. And, to everyone's benefit, the company argued, it would expand the tax base and make room for even more houses. "Unless we can do that it destroys our ability to develop," according to Charles Kane, an executive with GAC properties.[73]

The project was never built. Among the obvious impediments was the fact that the land was only one meter above mean sea level and subject to seasonal flooding, but what really scotched the deal was a black swan event: the oil supply crisis of 1973.

In October, OPEC decided to embargo crude oil exports to all countries supporting Israel in the Yom Kippur War. The United States was at the top of the list. While the embargo lasted only six months, the price of gasoline at the pump increased over 40% and the effect on aviation gas was even greater. Since GAC sold much of its land using its own airplanes, it had to severely curtail operations.

The oil crisis threw the world into a deep recession. Unemployment in the United States went from 4.5% to 8.4%. Economic activity declined and the real estate market for Florida properties dried up. Increasing interest rates added to the company's cost of capital, and faced with mounting financial pressures the company filed for Chapter 11 reorganization in 1975.

STATE STEPS IN

With a new source of funds available from the EEL program GAC Properties offered to sell its holdings to the state, but the penalty for Gulf American's overdredging in Cape Coral interfered, so the company agreed to trade 9,523 acres north of US41 in lieu of a cash fine.

In May 1973, the state accepted GAC's offer. The 9,523 acres was less than the 20,000 originally proposed, but it jump-started the process of land acquisition. The Conservancy then transferred title to another 2,000 acres given it by a board member, and the following year the Florida Internal Improvement Fund (IIF) authorized another 24,500 acres at $179 an acre. With that, the Fakahatchee was designated as a State Park. Hunting was no longer allowed. Private owners were solicited and a few sold their holdings, but the price was going up so most held on for the ride, even though being a state park would severely curtail development.

The pace of purchases picked up. In 1976, the IIF voted to buy 34,005 acres to add to the parcels already in state ownership. One of the Conservancy's founders, Lester Norris, bought 600 acres and built a 2,200' boardwalk for visitors to enjoy the raw beauty of the swamp. Natural Resources Director Harmon Shields indicated that the state had its eye on another 28,000 acres to fill out the preserve but prices were rising dramatically when another parcel, consisting of about 8,800 acres, was purchased by the state. The price was $382 per acre.[74]

By 1978 44,000 acres were in the state's hands; by 1999 it had increased to almost 70,000 acres, bought with Preservation 2000 funds, leaving some 16,000 acres still in private hands. The real problem was nearly 6,000 remaining inholdings. The strand was an inhospitable domain. Most owners used their property only on occasion, and over time became willing sellers as the state restricted hunting rights. But Marjory Douglas, the tireless one, was not there to see it. She had passed away in 1998 and Franklin remembers a moment toward the end of her life.

In 1997 Kathy and I went over to Coconut Grove to visit with Mrs. Douglas on her 107th birthday. We brought our friend Kathy Spaulding from Naples with us. Kathy wanted to meet Mrs. Douglas and possibly do a life sized bronze sculpture of Marjory to set in a special place in her honor. We brought Marjory's favorite ice cream, pistachio, to the cottage. Pistachio and cup of tea with Marjory became a grand occasion. Even though Mrs. Douglas was blind and hard of hearing in one ear, her mind was still sharp. It was a wonderful visit.

As of this writing there are still a number of inholdings in the Fakahatchee, but they are fading with time and as generations pass. An active friends' group has convinced the state to refurbish the boardwalk and build a new welcome center. Fakahatchee volunteers host swamp walks in waist high water, cautioning guests to avoid alligator holes and the occasional cottonmouth moccasin. But the indigenous population of small animals is on a decline from a voracious predator: the Burmese python. Once pets, as they grew large and hard to control, people released them into the wild where they reproduced at an alarming rate with few predators to cull the population. With all the effort that went in to save the Fakahatchee, the delicate ecosystem is once again being violated by man's unthinking carelessness.

Picayune Strand

In 2000 the U.S. Congress approved the largest eco-system restoration plan in the history of the world. It was called the Comprehensive Everglades Restoration Plan (CERP). Part of the Water Resources Development Act, it would eventually involve 68 different components. To be completed in 30 years, the cost was estimated at $7.8 billion. One project was to restore sheet flow of water in the Picayune Strand, also known as Southern Golden Gate Estates (SGGE).

The southern Estates, south of I-75, had been drained in the late 1960s by four canals, the Miller, Faka-Union, Merritt, and Prairie. The first two also pulled water from the northern Estates (NGGE) where several new homes had been built.

The main problem created by the canals, which eventually fed into a single collector just north of Port of the Islands, was that fresh water laden with nutrients emptied into the Ten Thousand Islands. The entire ecosystem was collapsing. The canals carried an increase of phosphorus ten times the normal level, nitrogen at five times, and ammonium at about double. Once the canals were built nature's great filtering system, clams and oysters, were unable to adapt quickly enough to the inflow and were stressed to the breaking point.

The need to do something was apparent well before the passage of CERP. While the land in the southern Estates had been drained, little broad-based development had taken place. A few families had built homes and Collier County was obliged to protect them. Fighting frequent fires and policing a 42,000 acre area where few people lived was costing the county a bundle, so county commissioners tried to front the problem in the spring of 1975. At a meeting attended by over 200 speakers and lasting well into the night, the subject of property rights arose again and again. The decision, as with many other controversial issues, was to kick the can down the road by appointing a group to study the situation and return with recommendations.

The committee was headed by Norman Bacon who, with the advice of Dean Maloney of the University of Florida Law School, worked out a soft solution that minimized the value of property rights law when considered relative to deterioration of undeveloped land in SGGE. It concluded that with increasing salinity of ground water and aquifers "... full-scale development of Golden Gate Estates would be the absolute destruction of Southwest Florida. You may not live to see it, but I can guarantee you our children will. Further development is wrong." [75]

After receiving the Bacon report, the commission was still twiddling thumbs as to how to proceed so it ordered up yet another study, this time an analysis of aquifer withdrawals and water quality in county well fields. The county's hired expert, Mel Lehman, found that as much as 100 billion gallons of saltwater had insinuated into the subsurface aquifers and opined that if the four canals remained fully functional the southern Estates would become a desert similar to the Sahara.

Adding another voice to the resistance against any further development Dr. Frank Craighead, named by Gov. Rubin Askew as "Scholar of the Everglades," told the Collier County Historical Society that if the southern Estates was fully developed residents would be visited by "...clouds of fine quartz sand drifting through every crevice during the winds of winter, by smoke from constant forest fires, and while in the summer mosquito control will be needed because of the intermittently flooded ponds." [76]

Desperate for a solution but frozen by property rights advocates, the county decided to use provisions of the Local Comprehensive Planning Act to rank the Estates into three classifications as to priority for development. The southern section was deemed unsuitable. The county requested that the Corps of Engineers figure out how to restore the natural flow of surface water and deal with 813 miles of dirt roads and 183 miles of canals—all falling into disrepair in the southern Estates.

The pivot came when the Federal Trade Commission forced GAC Properties into bankruptcy in 1980 for fraudulent sales practices. It had filed earlier for reorganization under Chapter 11 of the Bankruptcy Act, but this time was forced into liquidation under Chapter 7. The court-appointed trustee negotiated a sale of assets to Avatar Holdings in Miami, and as part of the final order asserted that road maintenance, safety and firefighting would have to fall to the taxpayers of Collier County. But the county had no interest in maintaining a virtually uninhabitable area. It was being used, with its long and straight roads, as a runway for drugs flown into South Florida. The few people living there were happily cultivating vegetables and marijuana plants, and the sheriff had little interest in messing with a situation that was causing few problems.

Adams describes one:

I remember one day driving over to the east coast early in the morning and looking down De Soto Blvd. where there was a yellow airplane parked on the street. I didn't think much of it, I didn't stop but on my way back that afternoon the plane was still there and was surrounded by sheriff's cars. In those days, before an interstate, you could just turn off the road so I drove up to see what was happening because I knew a lot of the guys in the sheriff's

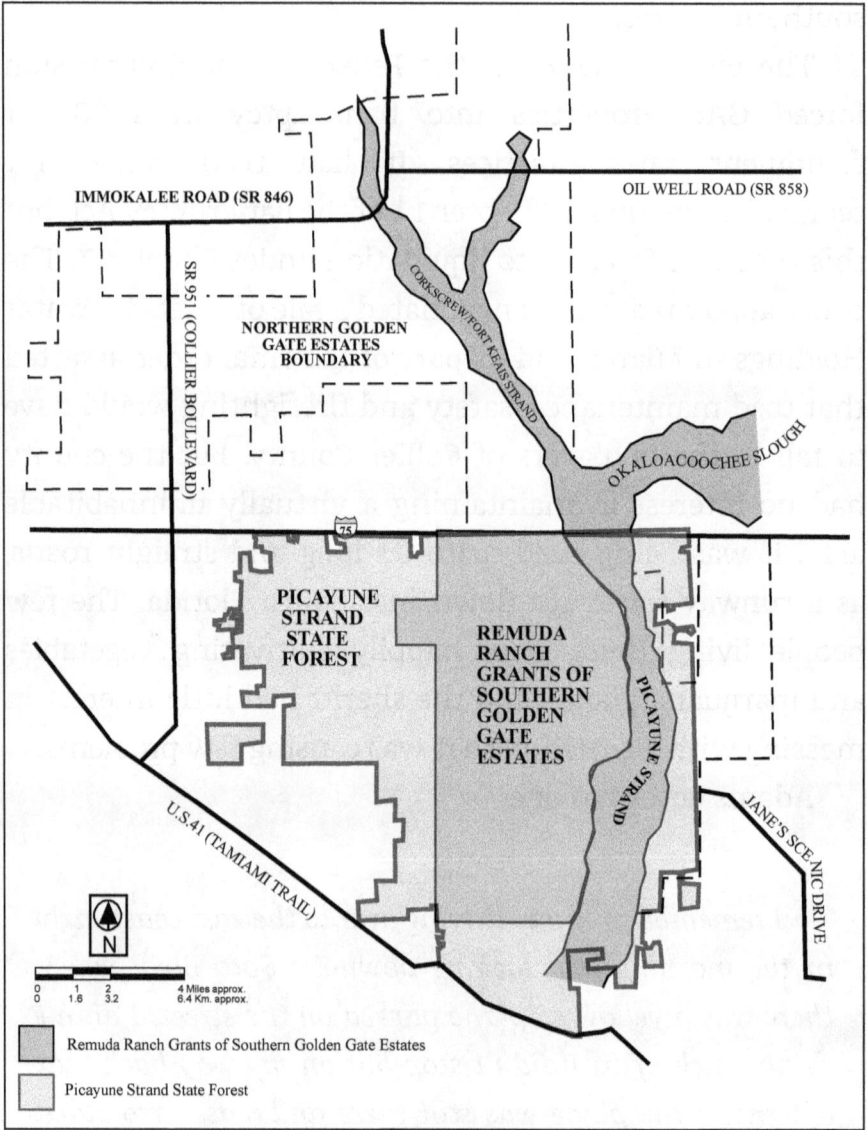

Picayune Strand and Remuda Ranch.
Map created by John G. Beriault.

office. When I got there they recognized me and I asked them what was going on. They said "well we just got a call about this airplane." I said "I went by here 7 AM this morning and it was here then," but no one would tell me what was going on.

The bankruptcy court order forced the county commission to look beyond study groups and deal directly with the future of the southern Estates. The main sticking point other than property rights was that residents of the northern section were uneasy. If the four canals below the interstate were plugged, they argued, their land might no longer drain during summer storms.

Finally the State of Florida intervened. A subsidiary of the South Florida Water Management District, the Big Cypress Basin Board (BCBB), recommended purchase of 50 sq. mi. in the southern Estates adjacent to the Fakahatchee. There was a question about funding priorities so the Conservancy suggested that the land be added to the Save Our Rivers (SOR) program, part of Gov. Graham's 1981 River Resources Act that would eventually preserve 1.7 million acres throughout the state because the 1979 Conservation and Recreation Lands (CARL) program, used for similar purchases, had limited funding at the time and the Estates were low priority, but as soon as the idea surfaced full-blown opposition to using SOR funds erupted in the form of an organization called the Land and Water Management Council of Collier County with Paul Kruse as Executive Director. His wife Mary-Frances had been elected to the Collier County Commission in 1980, and they owned a newspaper called the *Golden Gate Eagle*, giving them a significant megaphone with which to oppose purchase. As the back-and-forth continued at the local level, a frustrated William Merrihue president of the Conservancy, wrote Sen. Lawton Chiles that "...the situation is a problem far beyond our capability to solve without federal help."[77] Chiles responded by getting the Senate Appropriations Subcommittee on Energy and Water Resources to fund a Corps study beginning in 1982.

County commissioners were relieved to have the feds take control of the situation. It gave them great political cover, and they continued to quietly support the idea of rehydration because while the cost of maintaining roads in the southern Estates was minimal, the annual cost of fighting fires was annually exceeding $1 million. Even more important politically was the continued involvement of the BCBB because it tied the project into the SFWMD which had taxing powers and a big budget.

In 1986 the Corps study was released. It recommended that the two eastern canals, the Merritt and Prairie be plugged from where they originated at the two-lane Everglades Parkway. A series of weirs would be built to levels that would spread seasonal rains out more evenly and create sheet flow to the Ten Thousand Islands and

Fakahatchee Bay. Some of the cost burden would be shifted from the state to the federal government because the Department of Transportation had decided to upgrade the highway into an interstate, requiring a DOT buyout of landowners due to the adverse effect on property values by depriving access to the highway.

With the Corps study in hand, and the feds paying a part of the cost, a consortium of conservation organizations again petitioned both Gov. Graham and the SFWMD board to use the Save our Rivers Act. The law was clear they argued. It specified that the land purchased would have to be sensitive and put to public use. The water management district had funds available; what it lacked was sufficient interest in the project.

In August 1986, during the waning days of Graham's administration, the Department of Environmental Regulation used the Corps study to appoint another group to prepare an action plan for hydrologic restoration. Known as the Committee on the Restoration of Golden Gate Estates it took an entirely different tack and recommended that the land be added to the original ACSC. That would place a higher threshold on development and push it up on the state's CARL priority list.

The ACSC program was part of the Florida Environmental Land and Water Management Act of 1972, the same bill that created the state's five water management districts. It was "...intended to protect resources and public facilities of major statewide significance, within the designated geographic areas, from uncontrolled development that would cause substantial deterioration of such resources."[78] It set out a series of rules, one of which was that the county's land development code had to provide that all permitting in the ACSC would have to be submitted for approval by the state.

The Big Cypress area of concern, created in 1973, was huge. It covered nearly 60% of Collier County and protected all of the Okaloacoochee Slough and a part of the Fort Keais Strand, both major flow ways. It also covered a part of the eastern rural lands, used mainly for agriculture at the time but also ripe for development.

In a conversation Adams offered greater detail:

> Well quite a few people had bought land in the Picayune from the Rosen brothers and there were tree farms and agriculture and a lot of uses. The people downstream in Rookery Bay were upset about what was coming down to them on the coast. They started talking about maybe buying the property out, but that is not something that people owned the property wanted. It was nasty. I have a couple letters to Gov. Graham about asking for help. Now who was the driving force, I'm not sure. The Conservancy was involved and Audubon was in the end I don't recall exactly who. There were just a lot of people talking, conservation minded people, saying you can't have water flowing from Corkscrew Swamp down to

Rookery Bay that way. There were millions of gallons of water a day coming into that area and it was destroying the ecosystem.

When the committee met for public comment at the Golden Gate community center it was confronted by a large and angry group of landowners convinced that the state wanted to buy the land to obtain mineral rights for resale to an unnamed energy company. Despite the public outcry, and after another series of hearings, the committee recommended that no more building permits be issued, that the project be moved up on the CARL list, and all private land be purchased within the next five years. The last was the tough one. There were over 17,000 individuals and corporate owners with some deceased, some out of business and many living in foreign countries. The state had few people to put on the project, so at the five year mark it had purchased only 1,300 acres.

The buyout slowed to a snail's pace, so the Conservancy stepped in and took over much of the clerical work with volunteers and interns combing through county records, preparing sales contracts to be sent to Tallahassee and forwarded on to landowners. The response was remarkable. Some 40% of those initially contacted accepted the buyout offer, but in 1988 a suit was brought arguing the state was not paying enough. As settlement the state agreed to reappraise the property and resumed attempts to purchase. A similar suit was brought in 1992 but quickly settled and by 1996 18,000 acres were in the state ownership. But there were still holdouts—a lot of them.

Part of the problem was that Avatar Holdings had continued to sell property to investors hoping to turn a fast buck if the state was forced to reappraise yet another time. As a contretemps, one proposal floated was for the state to immediately plug all canals and tear up all the roads. That would bring the price down and increase the incentive to sell, but the decision was to hold off until all land was in the hands of the state.

The Conservancy was beginning to lose interest because progress was slow and the lawsuits were keeping things at a low boil until a citizens group called Keep Collier Paradise got enough signatures to put a half-cent sales tax increase on the November 1996 ballot. It would generate $80 million over the next four years for land acquisition, but went down because of a notable lack of enthusiasm from county commissioners and a heavily financed anti-tax campaign.

After that defeat the county did an about-face. It decided to modify the existing comprehensive plan by canceling the section on acquisition and replacing it with a mealy assertion that natural resources in the county would be protected. But vague nostrums were not enough for environmental groups who were able to turn out large numbers of people, particularly during the "season," and at an April 1997 meeting commissioners reinstituted the section on buyout of the southern Estates with the agreement that conservation groups would keep pressure on the Department of Environmental Protection (formerly the Department of Environmental Regulation) and the SFWMD.

The breakthrough came in June 1997. Vice President Al Gore announced a $25 million dollar grant from the federal Farm Bill to purchase land in the Estates if the Preservation 2000 program would match the funds. The estimate was that together the two could buy as much as 62,000 acres, well above the amount in the southern Estates alone. It eased the financial burden for the state; federal money was available in June 1998. Adding to the momentum Avatar Holdings, after eighteen months of back-and-forth, agreed to sell 8,500 acres of land it owned.

Then two things happened. First, the dot.com bubble collapsed. As the stock market took a dive in 2000 many investors found themselves scrambling for liquidity. Second, the U.S. Congress passed the landmark Comprehensive Everglades Restoration Plan (CERP), and rehydration of the southern Estates was included as one of the projects. The pace of buyouts accelerated.

USACE PLAN FOR RESTORATION

After the passage of CERP, it took four years for the Corps of Engineers to come up with a final project schedule and accompanying environmental impact statement.

According to the report: "... due to its size and complexity, implementation of the CERP required that it be divided into smaller packages that are referred to as projects. Each project is studied in a finer level of detail than was possible in the conceptual CERP report." [79] One of those "smaller packages" was the southern Estates also known as the Picayune Strand.

When details of the Picayune Strand Restoration Project (PSRP) were announced in September 2004, organized and vocal opposition arose again from thousands of residents living in the northern Estates. Their fear this time was that by eliminating two canals it would lead to rainy season flooding north of I-75. In looking at plan they had a point since 42 of the 48 miles in the southern Estates would be plugged to allow water spread out to slowly south. Discharge during the wet season in Florida from the canals into Fakahatchee Bay would be reduced to 8,300 acre-feet from approximately 35,000 acre-feet. But the Corps had planned for that with oversized pumps that could regulate the outflow and functioning of the remaining Miller and Faka-Union canals.

Another objection was that access by off-road vehicles would be reduced by closed roads and rising of water levels in the Picayune, and that hunting would no longer be allowed. The last objection was met by giving the hook and bullet friendly Florida Division of Forestry (DOF) management of the land after the project was completed and allowing recreation including "... hiking, horseback riding, bird watching, hunting, and vehicle use." [80]

A second management planreaffirmed those:

"(It would be) ... managed in accordance with the multiple-use management concept to restore, maintain and protect in perpetuity all needed activities and now is working on some of which ecosystems; to integrate compatible human use; and to ensure longer-term viability of populations and species considered rare. Multiple-use management includes, but is not limited to silvicultural management, recreation, wildlife management, archaeological and cultural resource management, ecosystem restoration, environmental education and watershed management." [81]

The plan, in a number of different places, also admitted that private inholdings in South Belle Meade to the west would make total restoration difficult because development there had already fragmented wildlife habitat, and allowed the introduction of invasive exotic plants. While the southern Estates would eventually be brought into complete public ownership, Belle Meade would take a little longer, but would have to happen because while in the rural fringe of Collier County (where some development was allowed), it had a high natural resource value all the way down and into Rookery Bay.

By 2008, the state had completed purchase of 19,993 parcels with federal and state funding and, as part of the Water Resources Development Act (WRDA), Congress authorized funds for restoration of 55,000 acres provided the SFWMD protect water for "natural systems" before any federal funding could be fully committed. [82] Known as a water reservation, the rule was an integral part of a sustained restoration program.

> "A water reservation is a legal mechanism to set aside water for the protection of fish and wildlife for public health and safety. When a water reservation is in place, quantities and timing of water flows at specific locations are protected for the natural system. The necessary quantities and timing are determined using data which link local hydrology to the needs of fish and wildlife. All presently existing legal uses of water are protected so long as the use is not contrary to the public interest. If a project develops water above the amount needed to protect fish and wildlife, the governing board may certify the volume available for allocation to consumptive uses." [83]

The governing board adopted the rule after scientific reviews and public workshops, entering it into the Florida Administrative Code in July 2009. The rule protected fish and wildlife in the Fakahatchee Estuary where the Picayune drained, and reserved a small amount of water from consumptive use for restoration of the Strand.

The final project had three pump stations south of I-75, a tie-back levee and three spreader canals to allow water to ooze to the south. The Faka-Union Canal, one of the two remaining, fed into the larger Port of the Islands waterway and into the Ten Thousand Islands where it was a favorite place for one of south Florida's iconic and endangered species.

MANATEE REFUGIUM

Manatees used the canal on a regular basis during the winter, all the way up into the Turner River, and the initial Corps plan included a series of culverts to provide protection for a proposed winter refuge.

The Manatee Mitigation Project, budgeted at $505 million, was in the original Corps design but not initially funded. After a survey during the winters of 2009-2011 by the U. S. Geological Survey of coastal regions from Everglades National Park to Marco Island, it was determined the refuge was necessary to prevent high winter mortality due to weather stress. The gentle beasts, living along south Florida coasts, can tolerate water temperatures down to 68°F and the Port of the Islands canal had a temperature inverted halocline. In plain language, there was warmer salt water at the lower levels above the survival threshold for the manatees. Other passive thermal refuges existed along the coast but Port of the Islands had by far the largest population of manatees which at one count was 225.[84]

Additional funding was needed but there was a question of whether land-based runoff would upset the salinity balance. If so, the thermocline might disappear. The Corps was aware of the possibility and designed a spoil area located south of Port of the Islands protected by culverts, and included multiple deep pools to connect to warmer ground water during winter months. The pools, covering 10 acres, were completed in 2016 with small shelves on the edge to allow emergency removal. Two culverts were designed to open during the warm and wet months for flushing, and the north end would be closed during winter months to preserve warm water for manatees entering from the south end of the pools. A long-term monitoring program was begun in 2016 and continues to this day.

SOUTH BELLE MEADE

Immediately to the west of the PSRP lay South Belle Meade, another CARL project. It was combined with the Picayune by the state to create a single forest management unit to reduce the push back from sportsmen. More important, the two, in combination with adjacent lands, would function as an interconnected unitary ecosystem

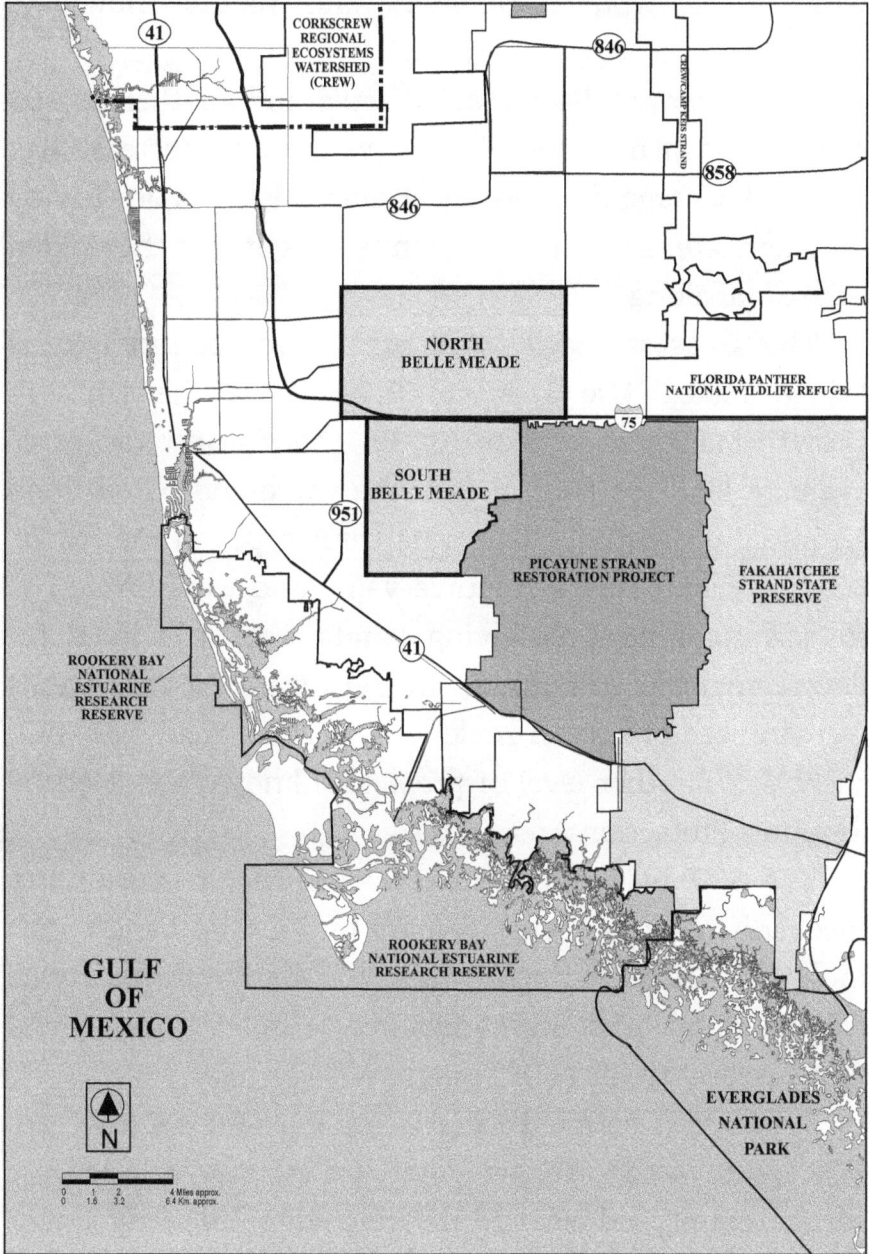

North and South Belle Meade.
Map created by John G. Beriault.

with linked wildlife corridors and natural flowways draining down into Rookery Bay.

Once restored, Belle Meade would add another 22,000 acres of cleansing sheet flow. It would also decrease wet season discharge into heavily compromised Naples Bay by moving water south rather than feeding it into the Golden Gate canal along I-75.

The areas set aside were part of the county's Rural Fringe Mixed Use District (RFMUD) in the county's Growth Management Plan (GMP). The plan attempted to evaluate land for natural resource value and based upon an initial evaluation there were three types in the fringe. Sending Lands had a resource value and were limited as to permitted uses. Receiving Lands were scheduled for development at some point in the future. Neutral Lands were in need of further review. Within the Sending Lands, there was another level of protection known as a Natural Resource Protection Area (NRPA).

The GMP was revised in 2002 and set up a voluntary mechanism for property owners of Sending Lands with more restrictive zoning to sell their development rights to owners of Receiving Lands. It was called a transfer of development rights (TDR) program.

When first adopted the minimum value for the base TDR credit was $5,000 per acre but there was little activity so the county added additional credits for early entry, environmental restoration, and a credit for land conveyed in fee simple to a federal, state or local government as a gift or as mitigation. The underlying concept was to allow the free market to set the price while respecting private property rights insofar as possible. Once development rights were severed it was permanent, with the exception of agricultural land abated for 25 years in order to prevent early conversion to other uses.

In South Belle Meade 227 people owned about 6,000 acres. In the north section another 340 owned 6,500 acres eligible for the program, but it was only marginally successful. There was little incentive to sell rights and even less to purchase them. The initial price also involved transaction costs, a fee to remove exotics and a perpetual exotic maintenance fee. At $5,000 an acre (with the underlying zoning at five acres) it was well below the market value of many of the lots so most of the activity was developers on both sides of the transaction who owned both Receiving and Sending Lands.

With a large part of South Belle Meade in Sending, and the TDR program marginal, the pace of property purchases by the state picked up and by 2021 all but four parcels were in public ownership and those were on the east side running down the edge of the preserved area.

A complicating factor to full restoration down to US 41 lay in the southwestern corner—a large operation called the 6L Farms. The Lipman family's operation makes it the largest field tomato-grower in the country. Begun in the 1950s, the company now has four farms, with the largest being in Collier County. The fields lie north of US 41 in the southwestern quadrant of the restoration area, and cover about 10 sq. mi.

The Lipman property is located within the historical flow way of surface water into Rookery Bay. In order to properly rehydrate while assuring that the water flowing into the estuary will not have additional nutrients a series of channels need to be established through the 6Ls. A large barrier to protect the farm from flooding has been built down the western edge of the restoration area, and a management plan is in the works. To control wet and dry season flows into the rehydration area would require a pump station and two flood protection levees to protect private lands to the south and west.

The Collier County watershed plan calls for two channels to flow through the 6Ls property, then through new culverts under US 41 and into what is called the Fiddler's Creek outfall system and eventually into Rookery Bay. To do that the county is working to "... develop a plan for this project that would allow the county to obtain the much-needed easements within the area over the next ten (10) years while not interfering with the current operations on the properties, and potentially benefiting the 6Ls group *if/when the properties transition to developments in the future* (italics mine)." [85]

Fiddler's Creek, lying east of CR 951 into Marco Island, was a controversial development from its inception. Originally platted for 2,379 acres with almost 6,000 homes and two golf courses, it was permitted when, after reviewing a private comp plan amendment, the Planning Commission agreed to add another 1,385 acres or 277 more homes. The project was outside the urban boundary at the time, but when the County Commission approved the amendment it moved the boundary line and gave Fiddler's Creek another four years to complete the project built right across the historic flow way into part of once pristine Rookery Bay.

The PSRP, authorized by Congress in 2007 for $375 million, would eventually rehydrate over 55,000 acres—or 85 sq. mi.—by removing canals and roads.[86] The state would buy and own the land, and the Corps would do the heavy lifting. State funds would come from CARL, Preservation 2000 and Florida Forever. The state then combined South Belle Meade with Southern Golden Gate Estates to form the Picayune Strand State Forest. It would be extensively monitored for progress in ridding the area of exotic vegetation and creating improved habitat for wildlife.

NORTH BELLE MEADE—NRPA

Separated from the Picayune and somewhat isolated on the east by the Miller Canal and Boulevard, on the north by the Golden Gate Canal, and on the west by Collier Boulevard lay North Belle Meade. The eastern half was a designated NRPA of about 10,500 acres. It was not included in the northern Estates in the 1960s, so there was little housing and few paved roads; it was isolated from the larger southern section by I-75. Zoning for the Sending Lands was one dwelling per 40 acres. The east section had 140 owners of 760 parcels. The west half was also in Sending but not designated as a NRPA because it was bordered on the west by significant development. It had 271 owners of 373 parcels. Many were developers expecting to use them as TDR credits.

The two sections were bifurcated by a corridor running down along the sides of Wilson Boulevard. Being part of the Rural Fringe the county allowed villages to be built, but insisted they be located where access to arterial or collector roads either existed or was planned (a source of ongoing controversy). The underlying density was standard: one dwelling per 5 acres with higher levels in villages. The corridor covered about 1,200 acres with 45 owners and 60 parcels, mostly investors expecting to build commercial facilities along Wilson.

The RFMUD remains under constant scrutiny because of the growing number of strip malls and gated communities between Collier and Everglades Boulevards and their impact on the quality of water going into the large estuary to the south. The 10 sq. mi. of Lipman property will be developed, so it is the steps taken now that are absolutely critical to the long-term health of Rookery Bay and the Ten Thousand Islands.

Now totaling over 110,000 acres, they were saved decades ago by Audubon and the Conservancy beginning in the 1960s. That story began with a "road to nowhere" planned to run down a chain of barrier islands with hotels and high rises closely resembling Miami Beach. The battle against the road was conducted by a few wealthy citizens in Naples, well before the jetport controversy, and led to formation of today's influential and powerful Conservancy of Southwest Florida. It is for that story we now turn the clock back to 1964.

Rookery Bay

Rookery Bay was occupied by small groups of pre-Columbian people beginning about 5,500 years ago. The watershed once consisted of over 127,000 acres with Henderson Creek as the main freshwater tributary. The estuary was protected by a chain of barrier islands all with sandy white beaches. They formed the northern edge of what would be later known as the Ten Thousand Islands. The original 195 sq. mi. had been reduced by a canal, by development in the northern Estates, and by the interdiction of sheet flow from the Everglades Parkway, now I-75. A proposal was made to build a ten-mile road from present day Bayshore Drive, south down along Keewaydin Island and, using a series of causeways, down Holloway, Cannon and Johnson Islands. It would then turn east and cross a bridge to tie into Marco Island, a long coastal strip running along the beaches with high-rise buildings dotted throughout the islands.

With a unanimous vote the county planning board recommended approval of the road and sent it along to the county commission for its March 1964 meeting. To appear at the meeting George Vega, a young attorney, had been retained by Laura and Lester Norris, Keeywadin Island's largest landowners who believed the road would open the island to cars and destroy its pristine habitat. They also enlisted Joel Kuperberg, who was on the Naples City Council at the time and manager of Caribbean Gardens. At the meeting Kuperberg described the importance of the coastal barrier islands to the overall health of the ecosystem and after his remarks unrolled petitions pasted together down the aisle of the commission chambers. Forty feet long, the document contained signatures from over 2,000 citizens. With that the commissioners voted the road down leaving Vega, Kuperberg and the Norris's to work out a way to prevent a recurrence of the proposal. They knew that things had a way of coming back—again and again.

Public ownership was really the only solution. Conservation easements were difficult to obtain and sometimes ephemeral. In order to raise sufficient funds to buy land in Rookery Bay a group of prominent and wealthy citizens from Port Royal formed the Collier County Conservancy in April 1964. With the assistance of Vega, the group catalogued ownership of islands down to Chokoloskee and Everglades City, the one-time county seat and initial base for Barron Collier's company. A second step was to fix the bulkhead line location because laws affecting

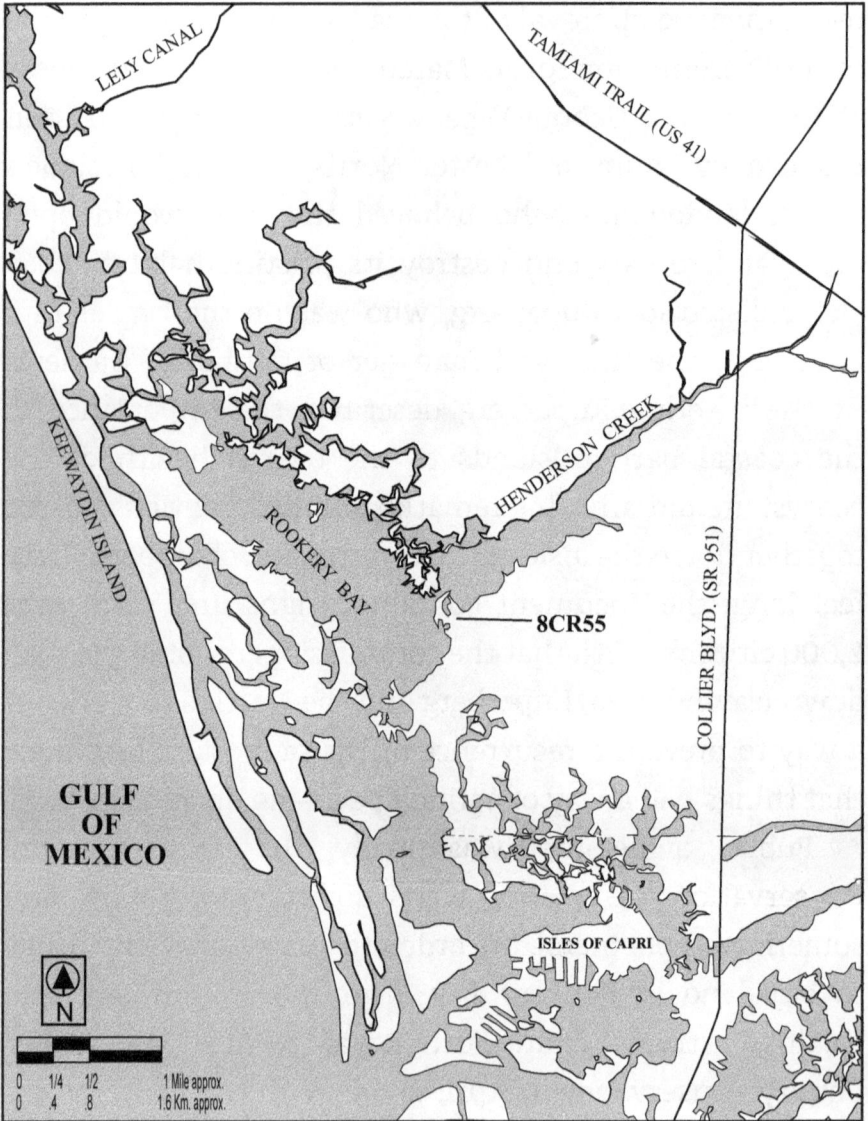

LELY CANAL

TAMIAMI TRAIL (US 41)

HENDERSON CREEK

KEEWAYDIN ISLAND

ROOKERY BAY

8CR55

COLLIER BLVD. (SR 951)

**GULF
OF
MEXICO**

ISLES OF CAPRI

N

| 0 | 1/4 | 1/2 | 1 Mile approx. |
| 0 | .4 | .8 | 1.6 Km. approx. |

Henderson Creek.
Map created by G. Beriault.

dry land above mean high tide were entirely different from those below. Initiated by the Bulkhead Act of 1957 it allowed local governments, after state approval, to issue building permits within a clearly defined line outside of which there could be no dredging. The act also gave title to submerged lands to the trustees of the Florida Internal Improvement Fund composed of the governor and cabinet officers. The act was amended in 1964 when Collier County set a line accepted by the state.

Kuperberg and Vega approached Barron Collier Jr. about putting his company's holdings in Rookery Bay, those inside the bulkhead line, up for sale. The proposal was initially rebuffed and in reaction the Conservancy decided to petition the county to move the bulkhead line further back from Naples down 70 miles to encompass all the barrier islands, but leave Marco out where the Deltona Corporation already had permits, and Collier had a piece of the action. The county commission accepted the proposal, but three months later reversed itself and moved the line outward to open up Henderson Creek, the main tributary feeder of Rookery Bay, for development.

In November 1964, Herb Mills, an official of the National Audubon Society, visited Caribbean Gardens, at the time a major attraction for visitors. His guide was Joel Kuperberg, who knew that the Audubon Society had a fund set aside for the acquisition of wetlands. After the tour Kuperberg brought up the subject of Audubon helping buy out some of the Collier holdings. Mills agreed to match money dollar for dollar raised by the Conservancy for the purchase if it would be designated as an Audubon Sanctuary. Negotiations with the Colliers lasted for weeks until an agreement was reached to purchase 2,600 acres for $300,000, 60% of the initial asking price. This was an indication to Kuperberg and others that the Collier family and its representatives might be flexible, par about the sale of their holdings particularly since exposure to storms made coastal development a less certain proposition as compared to inland property. Kuperberg's intuition was good; the Collier family was willing to work out deals if the price was right and in some cases donated large tracts without compensation.

The effort raised $400,000 from over 1,400 citizens and businesses when in April 1967 the planning commission, controlled at the time by development interests, quickly approved another massive project. Designed by a consulting firm hired by the commission for $15,000, it was another road that would run for twenty miles beginning at rapidly growing Marco Island down along the coast passing over the Blackwater, Wood and Fakahatchee Rivers. It would leapfrog across a few small islands and end at Carnestown at the intersection of the Tamiami Trail and SR 29. The idea was to attract buyers and visitors with an easy drive from urbanizing Miami and the east coast to pristine shores bordered by high rises built near sandy beaches. It was scheduled to be an amendment to the county's comprehensive plan, the document guiding all future development.

Once again, public opinion went heavily against the road and the county commission, at a public hearing, scotched the idea for good.

The 2,600 acres, the original 1,600 and 1,000 at Henderson Creek (despite ongoing pollution problems), were ceremoniously transferred to the National Audubon Society in January 1968. The State of Florida added another 1,400 acres of submerged and jurisdictional wetlands, and attention turned to how to manage the new acquisition.

ROOKERY BAY AREA PROJECT STUDY

Buying land was one thing; overseeing it was another. In an attempt to work from a science base the Conservancy engaged the Conservation Foundation to do a study of how to manage an estuary set aside for public use. Funded by the Ford Foundation, it was overseen by Russell Train, later the first Secretary of Environmental Protection Agency under President Nixon. It was presented to the county commission and a group of major landholders in May 1968 with five recommendations: first, to designate or create a single government entity controlling development of lands adjacent to the estuary; second, carefully control point source pollution and strictly regulate pesticides and fertilizers in the drainage basin; third, maintain free-flowing and open waterways to allow flushing and tidal changes to maintain health of the fringe mangroves;

fourth, to use principles of good development with clustered housing; fifth, mandate that all barrier islands fronting Rookery Bay be accessible only by boat. The study concluded with an admonition: early adoption of the five principles, with strict enforcement, was necessary to preserve the estuary.

It was greeted by Norman Herren, general superintendent of the Collier Company, with a carefully worded comment: "We would give sincere consideration to any information provided us that would tend to create harmonious development of the Collier holdings in the Rookery Bay area." [87] However, "harmonious development" was not what the Conservancy had in mind. Then, the commission, in a stunning reversal of form, accepted the recommendations and went so far as to set out mitigation procedures for areas already corrupted by development.

One of the "Collier holdings" of great interest to the Conservancy was along the shores of Henderson Creek, the main river flowing into Rookery Bay, an integral part of the ecosystem and as critical to its health as the flow from Belle Meade and the rural fringe.

HENDERSON CREEK

The bulkhead line along the creek had been moved back in 1967 to open up land along the creek for development with little attention paid to the possibility of polluted runoff. Charles Draper, a devoted fisherman and retired Air Force colonel, was one of the major donors behind a 1,000 acre purchase of land adjacent to the mouth and lower parts of the creek. It was a Class II water body—the site of a large commercial oyster harvesting operation that dated back to 1954, but Draper believed the creek, which emptied into Rookery and Johnson Bays, was severely polluted. He was right, and the Collier County Health Department, once notified, decided to close it in March, 1968 to taking of any shellfish due to high concentrations of pollutants and *e coli*. But closing the creek to shell fishing would do little for the overall health of Rookery Bay unless the sources of the problem could be clearly established. To do that, the Conservancy hired Black, Crow and Eidsness, an engineering firm from Gainesville specializing in water quality work.

Three weeks later, it reported back that "pollution is highest at the Kenyon Trailer Park outfall."[88] The trailer park sewer treatment system was permitted for 90 hookups or 9,000 gallons per day; while doing their sampling, the engineers estimated between 125 and 150 trailers were parked on pads and fully hooked up.

Violations continued the following year bringing the National Audubon Society, designated to hold title to all lands purchased in Rookery, to insist the county establish and make public the results of a regular sampling program. It did, but the data was buried in the bureaucracy and hard to obtain—leading to even greater frustration.[89]

At that point, the Conservancy made a critical decision. Impressed by the work of the Conservation Foundation, it decided that the best way to identify ongoing pollution was not to hire outside consultants to do occasional studies, but to create a science department capable of regular, ongoing monitoring, and had the land for a lab facility: 44-acres at the end of Shell Island Road adjacent to an archeological site—8CR55. Renovation of an older home was paid for by the Norris family and eponymously named the Norris Marine Research Laboratory. Located at water's edge, fronting a small basin created by excavation of a prehistoric shell mound on the south side of Henderson Creek as it emptied into Halls Bay, it was an ideal base from which to study the level of pollutants in Rookery Bay. The goal was crystal clear: "We want to know what is the state of waters in Rookery Bay and Henderson Creek and who is doing what to our beautiful bay." [90] But there was more to it—much more.

Southwest Florida was growing rapidly but maintained an essentially rural mentality, a general suspicion of government and willingness to overlook the obvious. It was reluctant to recognize the environmental effects of urbanization. Collier County had established a Coastal Area Planning Advisory Committee populated by appointees with close ties to the development community. There was no internal county planning staff. That was done by consultants, many of whom had conflicted allegiances. Land use decisions were made on a case-by-case basis depending, to some extent, on personal relationships, all against a background of state agencies just beginning to work through the early spate of growth management laws.

The Norris Lab study, staffed by a scientist from the University of Miami, began sampling in Rookery Bay proper by installing tidal amplitude stations and sediment traps at tidal openings. Water samples were measured over time for copper, chromium fluoride, various phosphates, nitrogen, pH, turbidity, and dissolved oxygen. Main purpose of the program was to establish a record over time of chemicals coming from developed lands adjacent to the bay and its feeder streams.[91]

As data accumulated from stations near the mouth of Henderson Creek it confirmed what was already known. The stream was a major source of pollution, and there was a point source: Kenyon Trailer Park.

Trailer parks in Collier County were permitted for a limited number of spaces—invariably exceeded by a factor of two or three times during the winter. And, until regular data collection was in place nothing would be done about it except under duress. As an example of overlooking the obvious, the State Board of Health and Florida Department of Air and Water Pollution Control came down in the middle of the summer to take a peek at the trailer pads and inspectors concluded there was no problem. The state counted 34 trailers in July, but the Conservancy revisited the park the following January to find 142 spaces occupied and hooked up.

Henderson Creek's problems were compounded by a 23-acre parcel purchased for development by Operating Engineers Union Local 675. In order to build the property up to resist storm surge, contractors had been hired to dredge the creek for fill. But the bottom of the creek happened to be state-owned lands. The activity was allegedly illegal, but the union assumed it would never be detected because at the time there was no monitoring system in place to tip off county authorities. The contractors had also dug up a small lake in the center of the property and connected it, via a canal, to drain directly into the creek. When county authorities were notified, dredging was discontinued and the canal was plugged.

Heightened concern led the Conservancy to convene a series of meetings with county commissioners, water district board members and staff, public and business interests, to hear presentations by Bernie Yokel, about the studies being done at the Norris Lab. Yokel was bright and forceful. He could be argumentative but his manner was matter of fact relying on logic and scientific substantiation. And he was effective because in October the County Commission passed a set of sweeping regulations aimed at preserving coastal zones with a transfer of development rights into lands more suitable for building. The county also initiated an environmental impact statement requirement for any development exceeding ten acres, and formed a task force to lay out a strategy for acquisition of land in Rookery Bay.

With change in the wind in both Collier County and Tallahassee, the Collier family decided to sell land at the mouth of the creek inside the bulkhead line. The price was $150,000. The Conservancy tried to talk the State of Florida into funding part of the purchase. Initial contacts were rebuffed but later Ney Landrum, recently appointed to head the Florida Department of Natural Resources, took a long look at the vast water wilderness, and began to promote the idea of incorporating Rookery Bay and the entire Ten Thousand Islands into Everglades National Park. That would require federal purchase, but a comment to the *New York Times* reflected the reality of the situation: "...inadequate Federal funding makes such a move impractical now and if anything is to be done in the foreseeable future, local interests and the state will have to do it." [92] But Landrum, known for his career devoted to the creation of Florida's modern state park system, would become an important player in the future.

THE TEN THOUSAND ISLANDS

Rookery Bay lies at the northern edge of the massive Ten Thousand Islands that begin at Cape Romano, located at the south tip of Marco Island and runs down to the mouth of Lostman's River. The northern part down to Everglades City is a National Wildlife Refuge and the portion from Everglades City to Lostman's is within Everglades National Park.

The system is fed by a vast watershed beginning in Hendry County stretching through Monroe County and into the Park. The main constructed feeders are the Blackwater River, Faka-Union Canal and the Barron River and Canal. The total watershed exceeds 1.5 million acres, almost 70% currently in conservation to restore natural sheet flows with the Big Cypress National Preserve and the Fakahatchee Strand combining for about 800,000 acres.[93]

With shell mounds as high as 50 feet Marco Island was the site of a large settlement with social complexity, art and ceremonial masks discovered by Frank Hamilton Cushing at an archaeological site known as Key Marco. Down the coast, navigating bays between the smaller mangrove islands was, and still is, difficult. Because of frequent storms and movement of sand mapping was difficult and only temporary. The bays are shallow, and since they are not dredged except for a few designated channels, tend to constantly shift. Many of the islands would connect to the mainland with a sea level drop of only 5 feet, but were mostly uninhabitable with the exception of Chokoloskee with about 500 residents.

Settlers moved in during and after the Civil War and some of the river outlets were occupied but only temporarily because of storms and limited fresh water. There were few visitors because the coast was populated by poachers and replete with moonshine stills. The people who lived there were tough and self-sufficient. The only means of contact was by boat. Fishing was an economic driver as was bird killing during the feather hat frenzy of the late 19th century, but by the turn of the century tourists were beginning to trickle in because of the sport fishing, pushing squatters south toward Cape Sable where there were fewer people.

Some of the barrier islands and coastal areas were later built up when permits were issued with little attention to environmental impacts and much more paid to the tax base created by additional housing and commercial structures. Ambitiously, the Collier County comprehensive plan at one time showed development along a road running down the coast along the mangrove forests with bridges all way to Key West.[94]

The story of preserving the coastal islands began in 1966 when the Phleny Daniels family living on Fakahatchee Island claimed title to 140 acres as a right of adverse possession. The island was on the south side of Fakahatchee Bay with a number of shell mounds. It was owned by Alico Development Corporation founded by the established Ben Hill Griffin family. The court's ruling upheld Alico's ownership but allowed the family to continue to live on and farm the island.

Three years later Joel Kuperberg, president of the Conservancy called his friend George Huntoon, a former race car driver, who was running part of the Collier family operations, to explore as to how Huntoon felt about the future of the company's coastal holdings. Kuperberg thought that the Colliers, and possibly Alico, might be willing to sell marginal land. In his notes was this:

"The Ten Thousand Islands came up in discussions with Doyle Connor and Fox Coulter (Chief Forester of Florida) and spoke to Huntoon and Herren at the IIF board meeting in Tally yesterday JK explained re: the Collier holdings in the Ten Thousand Islands indicating that someone had suggested that the Collier's might be ready to give the Islands to a preserve use. JK explained that the negotiations with Ney Landrum re: the state acquisition of the Alico holdings, pending federal legislation and disposition to acquire the entire Ten Thousand Islands through purchase after negotiations with the Colliers (per the many conversations twixt Huntoon, Herren, the BOR, and Fish and Wildlife people, and JK). This seemed to satisfy Huntoon. JK and Huntoon agreed to an early meeting to review the matter as both feel the idea is beginning to take shape and should be worked out more fully, before the Collier's hear of the idea through the back door." [95]

The idea went nowhere. Alico was not interested in selling and it wasn't going to happen until a level of trust could be developed—which it would over time. But many of the players were in place and would begin a protracted minuet back and forth with each other and the state legislature leading eventually to a very big deal.

Ney Landrum, who had been involved in the overdredging at Cape Coral and the problems at Henderson Creek, was executive director of the Florida Outdoor Recreation Council at the time. He was a reliable conduit into Gov. Askew's office. Norman Herren would soon become overall operating head of the Collier family's operations. Huntoon, over the ensuing years, would use his influence to help with the purchase of a number of small properties and became close friends with Kuperberg. He had been Herren's deputy at the Collier Company, a member of the county's environmental advisory committee, and was respected by the three largest landowners in Southwest Florida.

Kuperberg eventually became executive director of the state's Internal Improvement Fund under Gov. Ruben Askew. He had not given up on the idea of buying all of Rookery Bay and brought the Nature Conservancy into the picture:

> "I believe that I am in a position able to prevail upon the trustees of the Internal Improvement Fund to make this acquisition of all the lands within some 60,000 acres of land and water in the north and west of the holdings which the Collier County Conservancy acquired

in 1968. Conveyance of this parcel at this time would provide the necessary incentive to see the balance of the Ten Thousand Islands come into public ownership." [96]

The reply came back that the Nature Conservancy would pass title to all its parcels to the Collier Conservancy with the proviso that it would be later transferred to State of Florida.

But the legislature refused to appropriate funds for the additional acres and Kuperberg, who quickly tired of the bureaucratic nature of government work, resigned and was replaced by Joseph Landers. The Conservancy requested a meeting with the governor and Landers after recruiting the Naples Women's Club, Naples Garden Club, Izaak Walton League and Collier County Audubon, all loaded with registered voters. An immediate response came back from Kenneth Woodburn, who had moved from the Florida Fresh Water Fish and Game Commission into the governor's inner circle. He had done a study of Rookery Bay in 1964, was familiar with the moribund status of the acquisition, and willing to meet.

The back and forth continued throughout the fall and winter of 1974 until January when the state purchased a small parcel at Cape Romano. One week later, Herren, by then heading up Collier company operations, indicated that the family might be willing to sell 20,000 acres between

Marco Island and Everglades National Park if the price was right.

Once again, the deal hit the rocks in Tallahassee because the state did not have enough money unless it designated Rookery Bay as a State Aquatic Preserve and despite efforts by Landers, Woodburn and the Conservancy, it didn't happen. Word came back that developers, with deep pockets, were concerned that a preserve would frustrate their plans to build out coastal property, and legislators were listening to them with wallets wide open. With that the situation turned quickly into a standoff characterized by a letter from a legislator to a frustrated land owner:

> "My investigation of the proposed acquisition of land around Green Bay for a sanctuary has revealed that this is almost a dead issue. Problems encountered in seeking appropriate management to support such a sanctuary have apparently been too difficult to surmount. It is my understanding an agreement between the Collier County Conservancy and the state on management could not be reached." [97]

The frustrated recipient was a real estate developer from Chicago who owned land along Henderson Creek, but the real issue was never management of a sanctuary. It was the difference between the state's insistence that the Conservancy pass title to the lands it held prior to any designation, and the the possibility that the state might, as it had in the past, sell the land for development. The stalemate was finally broken by Gov. Askew who convinced the legislature to designate 58,000 acres of Rookery Bay as an Aquatic Preserve. In a parallel action the Conservancy, using the Audubon Society's good offices in Washington, had convinced the feds to name Rookery Bay as a National Estuarine Research Reserve, setting aside nearly 110,000 acres. The program, under the Coastal Zone Management Act of 1972, brought in Rookery Bay as the third bioregion in the country to enter the system.

DELTONA AND THE COLLIER-READ TRACT

Part of the Ten Thousand Islands was Marco Island, developed in the 1960s and 1970s by the Mackle Brothers and their Deltona Corporation. They were known in Tallahassee as good developers having done subdivisions in the central part of the state and Key Biscayne on the east coast. Immediately to the south of the newly preserved land and mangroves forests in Rookery Bay they purchased over 6,700 acres from Barron Collier, Jr. (who remained as a partner), took an option on another 3,600 acres and applied for permits beginning in 1964. And the Mackles had even bigger plans.

As the project grew Deltona set its sight on 9,000 acres to the north around Collier Bay also known as the Collier-Read tract. Covered by mangrove forests, it buffered the new and growing Rookery Bay preserve until it was purchased by Deltona. It would be incorporated into Marco Shores to the east to be built out with Venetian-style houses, the architectural fantasy of the era. 3,700 home sites were sold and construction was ready to go once all permits were in hand.[98]

Bernie Yokel, on staff at the Conservancy, took one look at the location and was convinced it would ruin mangrove forests in preserved areas to the north. His tactic was to delay the permitting process because legislation being debated in Washington would have a dramatic impact on the future of coastal development. And he was right.

In 1970 the Environmental Protection Act was passed, followed by the Clean Water Act in 1972, the Coastal Zone Management Act requiring states to make plans to preserve coastal ecosystems while giving the public access to its beaches and the Endangered Species Act in 1973. Each of those became a blunt instrument with which the Conservancy attacked the Collier-Read tract.

The dynamic in Florida was also changing. The 1972 Florida Water Resources Act confirmed that the state had the right to control the waters of Florida for their "full beneficial use" with the Department of Natural Resources having jurisdiction. In the same year Congress created the National Estuary Research Reserve system with Rookery Bay being an early entrant. While the new laws were moving ahead, the economy was beginning to stall and Deltona decided to temporarily suspend all sales of lots on Marco Island pending final approval of the Collier-Read project.

The Army Corps of Engineers would have to issue the main permit. It had the reputation of being easy on development applications and been sued by the Natural Resources Defense Council (NRDC) to ensure that the terms of the Water Pollution Control Act of 1972 would be scrupulously applied. When the decision came down on the NRDC suit, the court asserted that the Corps needed to take its responsibilities more seriously. The Corps responded by scheduling a public hearing.

It was held at Lely High School. Presiding would be Col. Donald Wisdom, district engineer from Jacksonville, also known as "the green colonel." A large and vocal contingent from the construction industry and Marco Island Civic Association filled the room to overflow. Deltona made the point that it had sold a number of home sites in other parts of Marco when permits were easy to get and it was all about past practices. But the most potent argument was that if a permit was denied it would amount to a "taking" of the land. Despite the threat, the Corps turned down Deltona's application and the company immediately filed suit arguing it should receive compensation for the loss, estimated at $34 million.

With the Corps' denial a number of buyers decided to seek refunds. The company offered to transfer title to other locations it was developing throughout Florida but most of the buyers had no interest in moving inland. To meet the demand, the company had to sell some of its commercial properties including its Marco hotel to the Marriott Corporation, but in 1980 the U. S. Court of Claims ruled that the "taking" was an "inverse condemnation proceeding" and that if the Corps did not revoke denial the company should indeed be compensated. Then, in January 1981 in another case, the U. S. District Court found in favor of the Corps forcing the company to appeal to the U. S. Supreme Court. It refused to hear the case.

With other avenues blocked, but the Claims Court ruling standing, Deltona decided to settle. The agreement called for all undeveloped parts of Marco Island to be turned into preservation land and for the Collier-Read tract to be transferred to the State of Florida and included in Rookery Bay (by that time declared a National Estuarine Research Reserve). The company was allowed to build 300 units on Horr's Island and a number of other units at Marco Shores, but neither had full water access and the company decided that buyers would not embrace those locations. Franklin Adams was deeply involved:

We almost acquired the island property from Deltona as it was on the CARL acquisition list. The Conservancy, League of Women Voters of Collier and several others of us did our best to get it moved up and purchased. I knew the Bob Graham's family veterinarian Elton Gissendanner who Graham appointed head of the Dept. of Natural

Resources. Gissendanner favored coastal properties for acquisition and wanted to acquire Horr's. He warned Deltona et al. to not rezone the island as the State would not be able to purchase it at a higher zoning. He said it was looking good. But then he called me the next morning after the bastard Collier County Commission voted to change the zoning, and said the acquisition was not going forward as now Deltona was asking more money. I am still bitter about what happened. The island was so rich in history, rare plants and it was discovered by archaeologists that Archaic people had resided there long before the Calusa did. It would have been an incredible park, but greed and politics prevailed.

While the Horr's Island development never took place the Conservancy, in the settlement, gained the right of access to make sure that designated preservation areas were not encroached upon as large single-family homes were built there, with owners presuming they had unfettered ownership of the entire island.

As part of the deal, the state deeded over 36 acres west of Miami International Airport in exchange for another 12,400 acres of wetlands. And with that, another 21,400 acres were added to the protected area. The land swap was a clear signal that the state was finally and firmly committed to preserving Rookery Bay. About 66,000 acres were then in conservation.

Title to all lands was passed to the State of Florida in 1980 with enhanced protective covenants. Construction on private inholdings in Rookery Bay was restricted and owners in the Ten Thousand Islands continued to either donate or sell their property as the state entered the 1980s with a series of programs, including Gov. Bob Graham's Save Our Everglades program, used to buy land and protect habitat like the Florida Panther Preserve. As more and more of the coast was protected, it became evident that uses would vary from scientific research to fishing to recreation, and various government agencies would be involved.

OVERLAPPING JURISDICTIONS

The history of coastal land and waters going from private to public ownership from Gordon Pass at the City of Naples down to the edge of Everglades National Park resulted in a series of overlapping jurisdictions. One of the challenges was coordination among government agencies. Of particular importance were state wildlife managers whose local knowledge would help design and create a workable model for both the maintenance and restoration of wetlands as well as travel corridors for birds and animals as the pace of development picked up and habitat fragmented. A review of each separate oversight follows:

The first level of protection was as a National Estuarine Research Reserve (NERR), a partnership between NOAA and the State of Florida. Established by the federal Coastal Zone Management Act of 1972, the system includes 29 reserves across the country protecting more than 1.3 million acres of coastal ecosystems. The mission is to provide for tourism and recreation, education and information, and the protection of cultural and historic resources. It is primarily a means to engage people in a process of hands-on education. The four Florida NERRs are managed by the Office of Coastal and Aquatic Managed Areas (CAMA), providing oversight of critical ecosystems.

A second level with emphasis on public access was the Aquatic Preserve (AP) administered by the Florida Department of Environmental Protection (DEP). There are 42 aquatic preserves in the state of Florida, one being the Cape Romano—Ten Thousand Islands AP running from the cape south to the Everglades Park boundary. Created by the legislature in 1975, the designation includes coastal waters "set aside forever as aquatic preserves or sanctuaries for the benefit of future generations due to exceptional biological aesthetic and scientific value." [99]

A third layer was the National Wildlife Refuge (NWR) system, administered by the U.S. Fish and Wildlife Service (USFWS), it covers vast areas of the United States and includes 568 refuges and 38 wetland preservation areas covering over 150 million acres. It is the world's largest network of public lands devoted to the conservation and preservation of wildlife. Founded by Pres. Roosevelt in 1903, it quickly gained the support of hunters and fishermen concerned with the decline of species due to overexploitation and poaching. Today the program is supported by a number of dedicated funds, mostly by the Federal Duck Stamp program where 98% of the user fees are spent on the purchase of habitat for waterfowl. One of those refuges is the Ten Thousand Islands NWR which overlays the State Aquatic Preserve.

Eventually the Cape Romano—Ten Thousand Islands added another 16,500 USFWS acres and would be merged into Rookery Bay. After being designated as an NERR it ended up with 110,000 acres of which 72,000 is open water, 31,000 tidal swamp and remaining 8,000 mainly in marsh, mesic flatwoods and about 2,200 acres of disturbed and developed land on Keeywadin and some of the other small islands.

An important lesson learned over the years was, that with a modicum of cooperation, marginal coastal and inland tracts could be purchased at a reasonable price for public benefit and use. Early on there were relatively few large landowners, mainly the two Collier companies and Alico, and they were in the first or second generation of ownership, most of whom lived and worked in southwest Florida.

Later, this would all play out into a decades-long effort to save an expansive wetland running from Lee County down to the Cocohatchee River and canal. It required cooperation from landowners who understood the need to leave parts of the native habitat untouched. It was called the Corkscrew Regional Ecosystem Watershed, and at the northern edge was one of the great wood stork breeding areas in America: Corkscrew Swamp.

Corkscrew Swamp

LOGGERS DELIGHT

Once the Fakahatchee and most of the Big Cypress had been logged to the point where it was increasingly expensive to pull the big trees out, and as demand was dropping following the end of World War II, the only large remaining forest was at Corkscrew where some of the trees, with their profusion of epiphytes and bromeliads, were standing nearly 100 feet tall after growing for centuries. It was owned by the Lee Tidewater Cypress Company.

Corkscrew is a "strand swamp, a water-filled channel in which trees are growing." [100] Once the home of between 7,000 and 10,000 wood storks, it was the headwaters of an entire flow system that ran through the Fakahatchee and Big Cypress down into coastal waters from Chokoloskee to Everglades National Park. Before roads and rail tracks were laid crisscrossing the landscape, it was a place of oozing water running as far as 150 miles to the southwest in a 50 mile wide swath much like the central Everglades.

What mattered most to Lee Tidewater were the trees, but what mattered even more to a group of committed citizens was the presence of a magnificent bird population.

SANCTUARY

Corkscrew had been protected going back to the days of the plume hunters, with seasonal wardens patrolling the property beginning in 1905. They were paid by Audubon Society members from the east coast of Florida who traveled by boat to Fort Myers to see the wildlife and earnestly desired to save it. Wardens were needed because plume hunters, increasingly frustrated by enforcement in coastal rookeries, found the swamp filled with birds and easy to access in and out.

Other than poaching, the area remained relatively untouched until 1952 when the loggers had finished in the Fakahatchee and Big Cypress. Corkscrew contained the last large stand of virgin bald and pond cypress in the United States, but cypress was being phased out by other building materials and the price was slowly dropping. Despite that, the company was ready to build roads and pull out the giant trees, as Adams remembers.

Randolph Swain, the Lee-Tidewater logging boss, was chomping at the bit to move into Corkscrew to log the last of the big cypress trees. The railroad, the locomotives etc. were just down to the south, and he wanted to finish the complete logging as they would never be back again. The equipment was sitting there, waiting for the go-ahead.

Despite Swain's readiness, he never got the green light. With pressure from Miami residents, and prodded after an article appeared in the *Saturday Evening Post* by Jeanne Holmes with photos by her husband John, a group approached Lee-Tidewater's president, Arthur Currey. He was willing to listen, and in a gesture of generosity, agreed to sell 2,000 acres and grant a lease-purchase for additional acreage. With the Collier family interests donating another 640 acres and funds raised from luminaries such as Arthur Vining Davis and John D. Rockefeller, Jr., supporters soon assembled 5,680 acres for what is today's Audubon Corkscrew Sanctuary.

One of the great stories of was about Mrs. Marcia Tucker, a wealthy dowager from Miami, major financial supporter of the Audubon Society, and a woman who would have a dry martini every afternoon no matter where she was.

"Before the boardwalk was completed, John Baker (president of National Audubon Society) decided to lead groups of potential donors out to the swamp on foot. One such group included a wealthy Miami woman named Marcia Tucker, an enthusiastic contributor to Audubon causes; she was in her 70s. The group walked through waist deep water and came out of the Corkscrew dripping wet but encouraged about the project's potential. After changing into dry clothes, they were taken by Jeep to the road where their cars were parked. The lead car, belonging to Mrs. Tucker, was a shiny, gray Daimler limousine. Waiting for her were a chauffeur and a footman. As the caravan made its way back to Miami, the Daimler stopped suddenly in front of a raunchy looking roadside bar in Immokalee, and the footman disappeared inside. Word spread that Mrs. Tucker had to have her favorite drink—a dry martini—every afternoon, no matter where she was. Minutes later, the footman reappeared, carrying a tray with a martini on it. Mrs. Tucker consumed her drink, then ordered a second while farm workers clustered around the car, watching curiously. Fortified by the two cocktails, Mrs. Tucker gave the order for the convoy to resume its trip to Miami." [101]

While logging operations were curtailed, fields around the Audubon property were being drained for citrus and row crops beginning in the 1950s. After two decades the shallow wetlands were drying out, changing forage vegetation for the wood stork population which depended upon seasonal wetlands and abundant small fish as food for their chicks. Water recession during the dry season was a critical factor, and something needed to be done before the wood storks moved north to Georgia. Deciding to go for the best solution, Audubon leadership in the person of Ed Carlson promoted the idea of a massive project to hydrate the sanctuary. To do it would require money—lots of it.

Franklin Adams knew that.

With regard to the Corkscrew, Joel Kuperberg asked me to get involved. But I could not because at the time was concentrating on other areas like the Kissimmee and the Turner River. And I knew that Ed Carlson would be involved, and he was a good person to work on that. I had previously been employed at Corkscrew Swamp by the National Audubon Society as a Warden/Naturalist beginning in November 1962.

Carlson was born in upstate New York. His family moved to Miami in 1954 and he soon became a high school "swamp rat."

"We were Everglades' explorers. We poked around the Big Cypress and the Fakahatchee and one day decided to drive SR 29 to Corkscrew. At that time the visitor center was a chickee shack and as we walked up dressed in camouflage and bare feet the lady asked us what we were doing. We said 'we just want to take a walk on the boardwalk.' The walk in those days was just a short in and out and while we were there, coming in the other direction was an Audubon warden dressed in full uniform. He said 'you boys behaving yourselves?' We said that we were and that we had always been looking for a place like Corkscrew. The warden said 'well if you're interested we need to do some boardwalk repair this summer. We have a dormitory and a Jeep that you can use.' And with that invitation, the day after I graduated from high school I was at Corkscrew. We built the loop on the boardwalk and I came back every summer after that and during spring break."

In graduate school at the University of Florida, Carlson took a course in environmental engineering taught by Howard Odum, a pioneer in systems ecology and a researcher into the iconic Florida springs. As one of the country preeminent scientists, he had received a large National Science Foundation grant for an experiment using wetlands for wastewater treatment and he needed a control site to compare to his experimental wetlands. He asked the class if anyone had any knowledge of Corkscrew. "I raised my hand, and he said come into my office right now."

After working with Odum, Carlson went on to do research for Audubon. He was named Director of Corkscrew in 1984, and shortly thereafter received a letter from the South Florida Water Management District. Addressed to a "dear interested party" it sought proposals for land acquisition under the Save Our Rivers Act. Any wetland system was eligible for funds. At the time there were three approved applications, the Indian River Lagoon, Kissimmee River area and part of a Water Conservation Area in the Everglades, but the district letter indicated that it was open to new projects.

"I thought, wow, what an opportunity. I got the paperwork from the district." Shortly thereafter Carlson received a phone call from Mark Benedict, chief science officer at the Conservancy of Southwest Florida asking about the letter. They agreed to split the work with Benedict doing the mapping of the area surrounding Corkscrew and Carlson writing the application. "We had no computers. All we had was electric typewriters. At least we could do corrections, but we just didn't have the ability to do mapping. The Conservancy could do that."

"Once done we took it over to West Palm Beach. The staff at the district told us that this was an off the charts good application, but they did not have enough money to do the entire project so said reduce the size and come back again. So I went back and redid the application for Bird Rookery Swamp only. But there were no purchases; it just didn't happen. However, there was a major drought, as I recall beginning in September 1988 and running well into 1989.

"The water supply was tight and people were talking about a moratorium on development. Coastal wells were turning salty. There was a board member at the district named James Garner from Fort Myers who represented development but expressed concern about protecting the water supply in southwest Florida. He was promoting this—the whole watershed. He thought it would make sense to do the whole project, to do it all. So Bill Helfrich called me up and said Ed, we're going to modify this and make it one big watershed."

CREW

Carlson was at his fishing camp in upper New York State when Kuperberg called.

"Ed, he said, I have a great idea. Instead of calling it a project we should call it the Corkscrew Regional Ecosystem Watershed or the CREW. With that, when I returned, I gave a lot of talks with my Kodak carousel of slides under my arm to local garden clubs, the Order of Eagles, and almost anyone who would listen to a message."

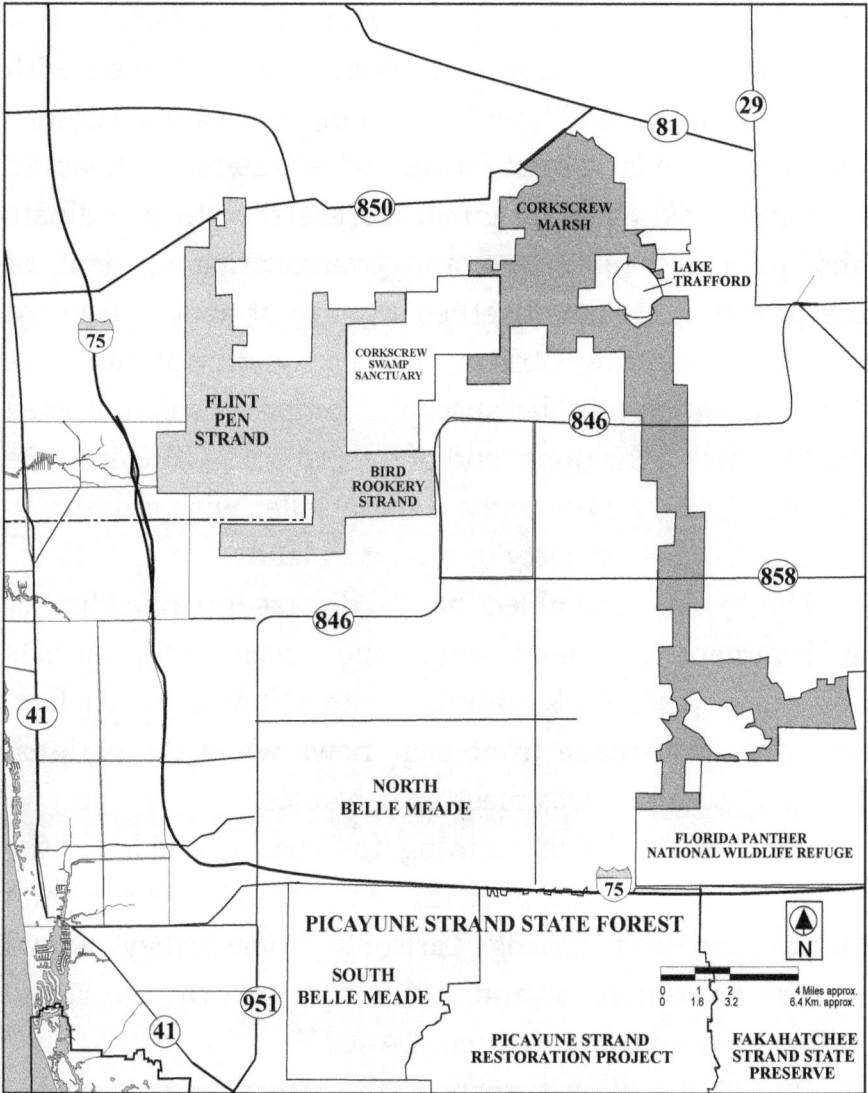

Corkscrew Swamp Sanctuary and Crew trust Lands.
Map created by John G. Beriault.

As the idea gained support, the water management district hired Joel Kuperberg to oversee the project. He had been director of Caribbean Gardens in Naples, then with the Conservancy and later Director of State Lands. His idea was to create a land trust for the entire watershed. It would be formed as a private-public partnership to coordinate and prioritize purchases and oversee management of the property. He put together a group of about 30 board members including Carlson, but the most important was Ben Hill Griffin, Sr. because his company, Alico, owned 4,600 acres on the upper end of the project. Buying into the group's vision, he became a willing seller with a desire to have part of his property in protected lands.

The group assembled had a diverse membership of environmentalists, landowners and developers, scientists and engineers. Alico's willingness to sell and put its land into the trust, made front page news while the national board of Audubon was meeting in Naples.

With Bill Helfrich running the district's side of the program, coordinating with Kuperberg's group and landowners and having Carlson's advice, they would prioritize properties and submit them to the Land Acquisition Advisory Council (LAAC).[102]

One of the main thrusts of the effort was to provide a wildlife corridor to connect Corkscrew Swamp with the preserve areas to the south. Initially the project was designed for about 50,000 acres with the emphasis on the Camp Keais Strand running from above Lake Trafford down through the Big Cypress into the Panther Refuge and Fakahatchee Strand but would increase with refined modeling.

Acquisition began with 6,700 acres, more than anticipated, purchased from Alico in 1991 using funds from the Save our Rivers program. Next, immediately to the south of the sanctuary, was Bird Rookery Swamp, the most important piece of the CREW to Carlson because some of it had been leased to hunters and he felt there was poaching going on. "It was a nightmare. It was important and we had to have it." The water management district asked Carlson if Audubon would like to manage the new property, but he declined having his hands full with management of the sanctuary. In 1994 an agreement was signed to have wildlife management and law enforcement handled by the Florida Fish and Wildlife Conservation Commission. The LAAC then initiated a matching grants program for any new acquisitions, using its partners Lee County and the SFWMD as partners.

The next piece to be acquired was the Flint Pen Strand on the west side of the rapidly growing sanctuary. County Commissioner Ray Judah convinced Lee 2020, the land purchase program in Lee County, to buy the strand and turn it over to the water management district.

The most controversial purchase in the CREW lands was the Pepper Ranch in 2009, some 2,500 acres bought by Conservation Collier Funds for over $32 million. The cost per acre exceeded any price to date, and stiffened resistance to the program on the county commission.

Carlson was concerned:

> "I went to the Collier County Commission, talked to Constantine and Norris and those guys and they said "we don't need to save any more land, we already have 70% of the county in public lands." I explained to them that what's important is that the water goes down to the Lower Tamiami aquifer. The water table fluctuates, so it was a very important recharge area."

The piece under discussion at the time a long linear stretch from Lake Trafford well down into the Panther Preserve and the Fakahatchee Strand, but the real problems lay at the other end of the CREW.

It was the Camp Keais Strand, essential to the initial design of the project, that would eventually end up being funneled into the Cocohatchee Canal after being squeezed down by a series of gated subdivisions along the north side of Immokalee Road and become a prime example of the problems created by fast-track permitting.

CUMULATIVE IMPACTS

The problem in permitting at the time was that each application was filed and reviewed independently with little or no analysis as to impact on the entire watershed from the top of the CREW to the Gulf. Even though the developments in question were at the very southern end of the Camp Keais watershed they could have a dramatic effect upstream as well as on the Cocohatchee River, listed as an Outstanding Florida Water, where no alteration was allowed that might degrade quality of the water body.[103]

When the National Environmental Policy Act was passed in 1969 one of the provisions was to take a broad view of the cumulative effects of a permit application. It was set forth in the statute as: "...the impact on the environment that results from incremental impact of the action when added to other past, present and reasonably foreseeable future actions." [104]

A 1989 Ninth Circuit Court of Appeals decision described cumulative impacts as: "...scattered bits of broken chain, some segments of which contain numerous links, while others have only one or two. Each segment stands alone but each link within each segment does not." [105] The decision was somewhat narrow, and offered defendants a way of curing the application to make it acceptable, but was another case where a slippery slope was created by fast-track permitting.

As suggested by the Leopold report on the Big Cypress, a better way would be to have a growth management plan with zoning strictly enforced. If not, each variance granted would become a new minimum standard, and each variance would encourage the next applicant to ask elected officials, many of whom owed allegiance to the wallets of special interests, for yet another few feet into a setback or an additional floor on another high-rise or a slight diversion of ground water flow. That was happening at the south end of the CREW watershed, with subdivisions being built by some of the most powerful companies in southwest Florida: U. S. Homes, Ronto Development and Bonita Bay Group.

To sort out the pieces, a suit was brought against the Corps by the Cocohatchee Coalition, a group of environmental organizations led by Florida Audubon concerned that the once twenty mile wide waterway was being squeezed down to no more than 200 feet as it entered a ditch called the Cocohatchee Canal running along Immokalee Road. After years in litigation, the parties reached a compromise in 2012 that would allow construction of a flow way of 800 feet and two water control pumps at Immokalee Road, but damage to the natural functioning of the watershed was irrevocable and done.

One of the last and largest pieces to be added to the CREW was Corkscrew Marsh—a coveted Alico parcel. The preserved area started south of SR 82 in Lee County which ran down the south edge of Lehigh Acres to abut both the sanctuary and northern border of the Fort Keais Strand. It was the final big piece, and thereafter the acquisition of land took place over the years, parcel by parcel, until 2020 when over 55,000 of the 60,000 acres identified as critical to the ecosystem were either in public ownership or land trust control.

The story of the CREW is not over. It's important because it overlays the Density Reduction Groundwater Recharge (DRGR) area, the main aquifer replenishment for a large part of Lee County. Numerous attempts have been made by mining companies to dig up rock for road building, some have been approved and some not but the county commission hasn't stopped there. For example, in June 2022 it approved a development for 10,000 new homes, and 700,000 sq. ft. of commercial space, in a 6,700-acre project called Kingston in the environmentally sensitive DRGR. It will be built between State Road 82 and Corkscrew.

In south Florida, there is always one more subdivision waiting to be built, and a quarry once mined out is a perfect setting for a lake surrounded by homes and a golf course or two as was the case at the bottom of the impeded CREW flow way and Camp Keais strand, so important as a critical section of the wildlife corridor. At the terminus would be a 26,000 acre protected area, won through long and hard negotiations. It was to become the Florida Panther National Wildlife Refuge.

Saving the Panther

Creation of the panther refuge is a tale of multiple moving parts, some synchronous and some grinding against one other. The story begins when the Ford Motor Company announced it would build a large automobile test track smack in the middle of Florida panther primary habitat. It would lead to a day in 1983 when Gov. Bob Graham announced his massive "Save Our Everglades" initiative. It involved an interstate highway interchange and a reluctant county commissioner that led the state and federal government to the eventual purchase of almost 165,000 acres of land into public ownership. And it would culminate with Graham's election to the United States Senate in 1986 where he, with Sen. Lawton Chiles (D-FL), co-sponsored a bill to "participate with the State of Florida in the acquisition of a 146,000-acre addition to the Big Cypress National Preserve." [106] And finally, the deal would reach all the way to Arizona.

FORD TEST TRACK

In 1978 the Ford Motor Company had warm weather automobile testing operations throughout South Florida, one in a West Palm Beach Industrial Park, and another at Naples Airport, and a number along public roadways. The tests were not so much for speed as for operational durability. The *Miami Herald*, in a small article in its business section announced:

> "Within four months. CMC Development Company will begin work on a $2 million car testing facility for Ford Motor Company in eastern Collier County. CMC, a division of Collier Enterprises, announced Tuesday they had reached an agreement on the project after two years of negotiation. Before work begins, however, the two must receive final approval from the Collier County commission, the South Florida Water Management District, the Florida Game and Fresh Water Fish Commission, the Florida Department of Natural Resources, the U.S. Fish and Wildlife Service, and the U.S. Environmental Protection Agency." [107]

The facility would be located just north of Alligator Alley and include Lucky Lake Strand and other low areas that drained into the Fakahatchee Strand to the south, already heavily compromised by the Golden Gate Canal and the southern Estates. It would cover 530 acres and include a 2.1 mile straightaway, a 2.5 mile oval track, and a 1 mile handling course, surrounded by an 8-foor high chain link fence topped with razor wire. Buildings would be no higher than 50 feet, and a 400 foot buffer zone would separate the test facility from nearby properties. It would require rezoning from agricultural use to a planned unit development with a 4–1 supermajority vote by the county commission.

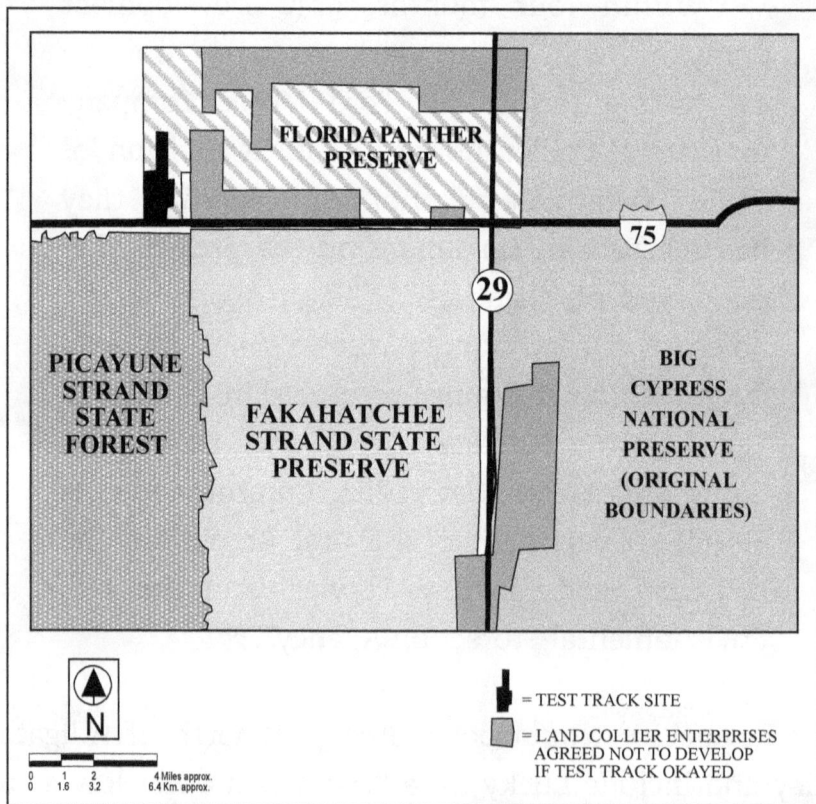

Florida Panther Preserve and test track area.
Map created by John G. Beriault.

Permitting was grinding along, and the business community was at full throttle. Collier County staff was behind the project and applied to the Florida Department of Commerce for money to repave 5.5 miles of Desoto Boulevard between Alligator Alley and Golden Gate Boulevard because the road was low and part of it under water during rainy season.

William Harper of the county's Economic Development Council said: "Payroll at the site will be close to $3 million per day and the employees have to spend money for housing, food and entertainment. Over 300 people will be flowing into stores and shops." [108] His comment was a bit hyperbolic; the actual impact was estimated at $3.7 million per year, not per day.

Fred Stevens, from the Florida Bureau of Business and Community Development was delighted: "I look at the Ford Motor Company as a bell tower for other clean, like industry. It looks just like the kind of industry we need. It is high paying, sophisticated and far enough away to not impact the area." [109]

However, not everyone agreed. In Franklin Adams' words:

In the beginning I organized and pushed the opposition to it. Because it was better habitat. It was wonderful panther habitat and not good for anything else. Certainly not a testing facility.

The U.S. Fish and Wildlife Service was also dead set against the permit:

> "The project area is within an area around the heart of the Fakahatchee strand that is considered important for use by some population of the endangered Florida panther. Article 7 of the amended Endangered Species Act of 1973 requires federal agencies to be sure that their actions do not jeopardize the continued existence of a listed species or destroy or adversely modify its critical habitat. We find this site is inappropriate for the proposed use, and we recommend you encourage the applicant to locate the facility on uplands at another location." [110]

Tom Lewis, of Wildlife Research, opposed the track because Lucky Lake Strand, only 100 yards from the project site, was used as a travel corridor by panthers. His objection was supported by a letter from the Florida Game and Freshwater Fish Commission executive director Robert Brantly:

> "The proposed straightaway would cross a cypress area known as West Strand, and the southernmost borrow pit would infringe on Lucky Lake strand. These wetlands were covered

with 6 inches of standing water during our field inspection although they had been dry during previous months the strand are part of the historic drainage area of the Fakahatchee strand which lies approximately 3 miles to the east of the project site. The strand and its drainage areas also provide an important source of fresh water to the Ten Thousand Islands estuary. In conclusion, we find the proposed test track facility is an inappropriate land use for the property which would cause adverse impacts to the area's fish and wildlife resources including many endangered species. Because alternative land sites can be found in South Florida, we recommend against issuance of this permit and that the applicant relocate this project to a more suitable location." [111]

Florida Audubon Society was even blunter. In a letter to the water management district Charles Lee stated: "This letter is in response to permit application 06273-D by CMC development Corporation, and application number 05263-A for the same project. We object to the issuance of the proposed permit and urge its denial." [112] Lee would play an important role in finally resolving the controversy, but his initial position was intractable.

Taking a slightly different tack Johnny Jones, Executive Director of the powerful Florida Wildlife Federation, went direct to Gov. Graham, pointing out that there was an agreement to limit I-75 interchanges from access roads in Golden Gate that would feed directly into the test track. His comments to Graham were prescient, because the interchange issue was top of the agenda for one of the county commissioners who would vote to approve, or disapprove, the rezone.

Ford's spokesman, Howard Freers, pushed back against conservationists saying it was outside the Fakahatchee Strand by 2½ miles at least and 1½ miles outside the buffer. He said that the track was designed to take advantage of the topography and there would be no canals or levees, but despite those assurances a permit application from CMC Development to fill in jurisdictional wetlands with approximately 10,000 cu. yd. of fill had been filed with the Corps in July 1983.

It became a public relations battle to win over the county commission when, amid the controversy the Coastal Area Planning Commission, populated by pro-development appointees, unanimously recommended approval of the rezone. With that in hand, CMC Development's consultant Wilson Miller went into full attack mode with letters to the Department of Environmental Regulation in Tallahassee and to the Corps in Jacksonville making the argument that it was a "clean industry" within the parameters of the county's comprehensive plan, that some borrow areas would be relocated out of jurisdictional wetlands, and that it's client's desire was to work diligently to get the necessary permits.

A full commission hearing was scheduled for October. Twenty-two letters were sent to the members from citizens in Golden Gate Estates who felt it would forever alter the wilderness area they lived in and loved. After six hours of contentious debate, the commission turned the project down by a vote of 3–2 (since rezoning required a supermajority). The Collier family immediately sued for $5 million based on the allegation that they were denied fair market value for the property and had spent significant money to get the agreement before the County Commission.

GOV. GRAHAM AND "SAVE OUR EVERGLADES"

Another of the moving parts was up in Tallahassee when *Sports Illustrated*, in its highly popular February 1981 "swimsuit issue" published a long article about the destruction of the Everglades and growing environmental issues in South Florida. The criticism was the brainchild of Johnny Jones. He felt that Gov. Graham was comfortable taking a centrist position on many issues, and was more favorable to agriculture even when its interests conflicted with the environment.

Graham had experience in cattle raising and was trying to seek a balance where possible. After being elected he realized that Pres. Reagan, with appointments of James Watt as Secretary of the Interior and Ann Gorsuch as head of the Environmental Protection Agency, would pay little attention to environmental issues and push decisions on budget matters down to the states.

Graham, despite being raised in a farming family, also knew that the public's views on land use were changing.[113] He was facing multiple choices on the location of a new jetport facility coming from the 1970 agreement on the Big Cypress. One of the sites selected was in Dade County and the local residents were howling. To deflect criticism Graham appointed a group of seven citizens to review the proposal, later announced his opposition to the location and subsequently withdrew the state from any further participation in the 1970 pact.

Water issues were becoming paramount and management of Lake Okeechobee was in need of better planning so in March 1983 he called department heads together to craft a master plan for Everglades' restoration, and became personally involved, holding a number of private meetings behind closed doors. He reappeared at an August press conference to pull the curtain back on a massive plan called "Save our Everglades." It had six elements, and included bringing the Kissimmee River back to its natural state with oxbows, meanders and riparian backwaters along the shoreline. The first project up was a big one—purchase, by state and federal agencies, of additional lands to add to the Big Cypress National Preserve and the Fakahatchee. Timing the projects was independent of the others and most of them relied on participation by the federal government to finance purchases.

MR. BROWN

One of the two "no" votes on the Ford test track rezone had come from Commissioner David "Doc" Brown. In another of Gov. Graham's selected projects, land would be acquired on both sides of Alligator Alley as it was being rebuilt into an interstate and an interchange at I-75 and SR 29 was pushed by farmers in his district to move their products to markets on the east coast. Brown was one of those farmers, and claimed his vote was based on an agreement that Audubon would drop its opposition to the SR 29 interchange, and provide legal assistance in the $5 million lawsuit filed by CMC development, if Brown would vote against the track.

SR 29 was Barron Collier's road and rail connection between the farming community of Immokalee and Everglades City. The problem for Audubon was the amount of development around a major highway intersection and the effect it would have on the endangered Florida panther. Audubon was increasingly concerned that with speculative money moving in the second vote to deny the rezone was in play because a number of parcels were being quietly bought up reminiscent of the activity around the Big Cypress jetport two decades earlier.

Brown admitted that endangered animals were not of great interest to him, but he knew they were to Audubon, and that informed his position: "The test track wasn't the issue to me. I was trying to make a trade with the Auduboners. ..." [114]

The Miccosukee Tribe was also against the interchange. The Tribe had been told that some of its property would be taken for right-of-way, but had been promised that it would have "...the only commercial interchange between SR 951 and US 27 in Broward County in exchange for some of their land. The tribe plans a gigantic truck stop on its reservation located at the Broward County line. It would be the first and only rest and service area along the 78 mile stretch of highway." [115] The Tribe also argued that the table had been set in the 1970s when Florida Audubon convinced Gov. Askew to have the Federal Highway Administration promise that if Alligator Alley was ever upgraded to an interstate, there would be no getting off the road until the Miccosukee interchange.

Despite the objections, in a vote for reconsideration, the county commission approved the rezone by a supermajority 4–1 with "Doc" Brown changing his vote.

Part of the reason, he alleged, was based on communication with an influential member of the environmental community. A director of the Conservancy of Southwest Florida, Ned Putzell, who would later become a Naples city councilman, had penned a letter on personal stationery apparently without the approval of the board indicating the organization's support for the test track. In March 1984 the Conservancy try to walk back Putzell's comments, but the commission vote had already been taken.[116] Adams felt he could have some effect but relented.

> *When the commissioners approved the track I was disappointed. I had a number of conversations with people from the Collier Company, Roy Cawley being the main one. In the beginning there was not a great deal of trust but eventually we were able to work things out in our discussions to the point that they were very amicable. I felt that the Izaak Walton League needed to take a stand against the track but I was just a volunteer and knew that there was some room for discussion but it would be better left to the professionals, people like Mott and Charles Lee and others. Those organizations had paid staff and they were the ones to do it. I was an unpaid volunteer raising a family and running my business, so at that point others needed to step into the test track issue.*

In early April Collier Enterprises announced that in exchange for Audubon approval it would place 32,000 acres into a land trust easement for ten years. Audubon, once strongly opposed, claimed it relented based upon panther research data and a comment by John Wodraska, acting director of the water board: "The state has indicated it would eventually like to buy that land. Everybody from the governor's office to the Audubon Society to our agency has been working on this. This could be an opportunity for the state to eventually acquire some very valuable, environmentally sensitive land." [117] Despite other commitments Adams could not leave it alone.

Purchase of the property would go a long way towards permanently protecting the habitat of the Florida Panther. Our organization, Friends of the Everglades, will do everything we can to support and encourage this purchase. But the test track should not be built there. As to the interchange that was still a big issue to resolve. Otherwise it was a good deal. The best outcome would be for the state to buy that land because the Colliers would have had a terrible time getting permits to do anything with that property.

The U.S. Fish and Wildlife Service and Florida Game and Freshwater Fish Commission also agreed to endorse the track if the county would agree to limit roadside services at the interchange. [118] The tentative agreement set forth a number of restrictions but left alone all permitted activities including leasing of oil drilling rights and minor modifications to existing facilities.

The deal was almost done when four days later the Ford Motor Company asked the water district to pull approval in order to work out further details on the one remaining problem: "Doc" Brown's SR 29 interchange. Charles Lee, who had been working behind the scenes to put most of the agreement together, said that the interchange was not part of the deal. The road would cut right through panther travel corridors where three cats had been killed in the last five years. Lee was still opposed but willing to reconsider.

One solution was to bring Gov. Graham into the picture, but his office remained strictly "hands off." The governor's silence was curious to the environmental community because he was becoming more open to putting sensitive land into public ownership. But what was not known was that private conversations were being held that would eventually result in a blockbuster announcement.

A NEW DEAL TAKES SHAPE

In late April 1984 the blockbuster was made public when Frank Logan, special counsel to the governor, announced to the press the state's intention to make the largest land purchase in Florida's history. It was part of Gov. Graham's Save Our Everglades package. Totaling nearly 165,000 acres it would include up to 37,100 acres in the ACSC west of SR 29 and north of I-75, and 127,758 acres both north and south of I-75 to the east of SR 29 and include an interchange. It was a complex deal with multiple moving parts, because the Reagan administration had put a heavy lid on the federal budget.

While the announcement was made under the aegis of the governor's new initiative, it included purchase of right-of-way along I-75—land owned mainly by the two Collier companies. This pleased Roy Cawley, representing

Collier, who commented: "The decision that I-75 would be a limited access highway with no interchange at SR 29 in itself would have unleashed thousands of lawsuits from voters who were promised access when they donated right-of-way for alligator alley. Then we faced a major uproar over development of the Ford testing track." [119] All parties wanted an amicable solution particularly "Doc" Brown. It was reported later that he was aware of the delicate negotiations regarding purchase of the area adjacent to the test track and had the issue ended up in court, discovery might have tied the matter up for years.

In addition to Collier Enterprises and the Barron Collier Company, which together owned over 65% of the property, there were another 5,000 small owners who had to be reckoned with, but once completed the buyout would serve to prevent any further development that could significantly alter the hydrology of the Everglades. [120]

The planned purchase stopped exactly at the eastern edge of the Ford site. When pressed the Graham administration's spokesperson, Estus Whitfield said: "To be honest with you I can't explain it. One thing for sure, if someone suggests that the section was left open for a Ford test track, the answer would be No! In all of our discussions when this was being drawn up the test track was never mentioned." [121]

The test track was obviously going to get built, so the need was to settle the interchange issue. By buying land along the right-of-way it would take the cost to the Florida

Department of Transportation off the table and preempt condemnation proceedings which would have ended up in court. Acquisition would have to stay ahead of the upgrade to the Alley and depended upon a firm commitment from the Department of the Interior to participate at up to 90% of the purchase price. The state would commit up to $16 million and the Ford Motor Company agreed to turn the test track site over to the state after 40 years.

USFWS PLAN

The next two years were spent buying out small landholders until 1985 when the USFWS released an environmental assessment of the Fakahatchee Strand. It included updated data collected from collared animals in the Fakahatchee as compared to the 1976 base line when habitats and travel corridors were reviewed for the first time. The assessment recommended purchase of three separate "units" all bordering the Fakahatchee to the west, north and east, and all within the ACSC. The biggest piece was on the northeast side of the Big Cypress but for some reason was not included in the study. Parcels under consideration, called "subunits," totaled 88,000 acres. The service was mainly interested in 30,000 acres north of Alligator Alley and west of SR 29 directly above the Fakahatchee Strand where telemetry data from five tagged panthers showed vigorous activity. The price, subject to appraisal, was estimated at between $12 million and $20 million. Most of the land was owned by Collier Enterprises.

In addition there were some private inholdings to the north, also part of the ACSC, and with proper easements landowners would be allowed to use their property limited to certain activities. Part of the proposed preserve had been leased by the Collier companies to a group called the Fakahatchee Conservation Club, and they were willing to modify the lease.

The USFWS plan emphasized the need to engage farmers and landowners and others like the hunting club in a cooperative effort to develop management practices that would protect panther habitat while remaining consistent with the needs of the landowner or farmer. The last was the most difficult because a number of farm animals, in addition to deer, were meals for the big cats.

The deal had already been made for 32,000 acres north of the Alley. It would become the Florida Panther National Wildlife Refuge. Collier Enterprises retained the right to sell the property but gave Florida Audubon the first right of refusal, a right that could be passed to the state. It would be available to Audubon or a designee at an appraised price. The SFWMD agreed to issue the necessary permits. Nathaniel Reed, instrumental in saving the Big Cypress, was on the district's board at the time and made the motion to approve with the comment: "They will be well paid. They will receive all kinds of glory." [122]

And, as a final touch, Franklin Adams wrote to Jack Lorenz, head of the Isaac Walton League of America:

"I think this has been the most difficult environmental issue that I have been involved in over the years. It was frequently frustrating and emotionally tiring to the point that I didn't want to discuss the issue or write about it by the time it was finally resolved." While I hated to withdraw our opposition to the test track from an idealistic viewpoint it appeared that given the resources of the Colliers and the politics of the total issue it would have accomplished nothing to continue our fight. As all the pieces fit into place we can be proud that the League had an intrinsic and vital part in bringing about what I consider to be a major victory for South Florida's environment and particularly the panther." [123]

For the second "subunit," the report encouraged the National Park Service to acquire an entire strip, approximately 15,000 acres, running along the Barron Canal between SR 29 and Big Cypress from the headwaters of the Okaloacoochee Slough all the way down to the Tamiami Trail. It was basically prairie habitat with a few cypress domes and mixed hardwoods, and had panther activity. Money would come from the Land and Water Conservation Fund, the primary source used by the National Park Service to acquire land from Collier Enterprises and Barron Collier Companies, along with smaller landowners. Approximately 15 to 20 residences in Copeland and Jerome would be excluded. The cost was estimated at between $6 million and $10 million.

Finally, the report rated the third subunit, the Picayune Strand, as desirable but only as secondary. Part of the reluctance to include the Picayune (or southern Estates) was the fact that there were over 10,000 separate owners, creating a logistical nightmare for buyouts, a conclusion similar to that reached by Collier County when it did an evaluation of the Fakahatchee a decade earlier.

For the land already identified by Gov. Graham as a priority to be added to the Big Cypress, the legislature provided the Department of Natural Resources condemnation powers to acquire parcels along SR 29 with money administered by the SFWMD and funded through a real estate transfer stamp tax. The only problem was that the district had already adopted a five-year plan for land acquisition, and no part of the USFWS study area was included.

So what happened to get the property was that 50 acres in Phoenix, Arizona I think was part of the deal. Somehow as I recall it was connected with creation of the Panther Refuge because it was all happening at about the same time.

Franklin Adams was right. To assemble sufficient funds another deal would be struck, this one to trade federal

Indian School Land in Phoenix, Arizona, for Collier land on the northeastern edge of the Big Cypress. Any additional acreage would be paid for by the state and federal governments. It all began when Bob Graham was elected to the U. S. Senate, and with his colleague Lawton Chiles supporting approval of a bill coming over from the House to authorize something called the Big Cypress National Preserve Addition.

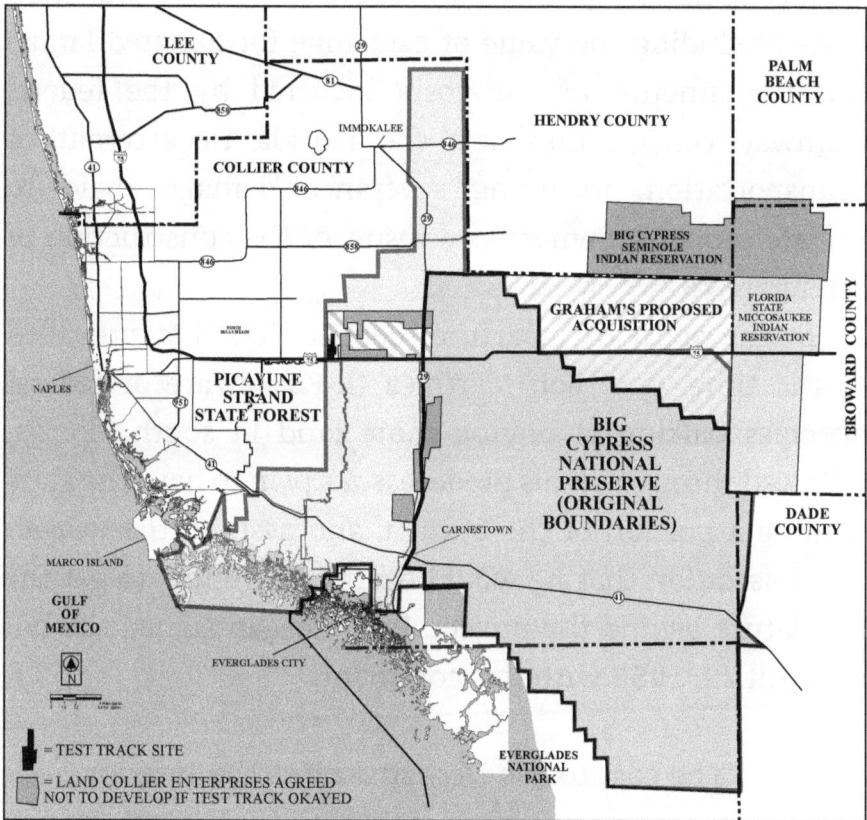

ACSC Big Cypress Preserve original boundaries and Addition Lands.

Map created by John G. Beriault.

ADDITION LANDS

What would become known as the Addition Lands at 146,000 acres lay to the east of the proposed Panther Refuge and south from the Seminole reservation down to the northern edge of the Big Cypress boundary created in 1974. The federal share, by Congressional mandate, could not exceed 80% of the total cost. The Land and Water Conservation Fund was tapped for $49,500,000.

Money already paid out applied to "the total acquisition costs (including the value of exchange for donated lands) less the amount of the costs incurred by the federal Highway construction and the Florida Department of Transportation, including severance damages paid to private property owners as a result of the construction of Interstate 75." [124]

In the spirit of bipartisan cooperation that prevailed at the time, Gov. Bob Martinez (R-FL), aware of federal agencies balking at buying more land in south Florida, followed through on his predecessor's plan to have the state assume a portion of the burden, and assured the Reagan administration that he would exert every effort to get the legislature behind the project. Pres. Reagan signed the bill on April 29, 1988 with this comment:

> "The cost to the Department of the Interior, for purchasing surface rights under the provisions of S. 90 would require $40 to $65 million in new appropriations. The Administration

has consistently advised the Congress that this cost is excessive and will oppose any appropriations for this purpose. To avoid this cost, and in recognition of the important role of the Big Cypress National Preserve in conserving nationally significant fish, wildlife, and other natural resources in southern Florida, the Department of the Interior has entered negotiations to acquire the private land to be added to the Preserve through an exchange with the private landowners. Such an exchange would require additional legislation, since the lands involved are in different States. I have been assured by the congressional delegation from Florida that legislation approving the Administration's exchange proposal will soon be considered by the Congress. I urge prompt passage of such legislation, which will not only provide the same protection that S. 90 provides, but also will generate Federal receipts of nearly $35 million resulting from the exchange." [125]

The state legislature quickly enacted a companion bill by appropriating up to $40 million for the Addition Lands to ensure that agreement with the federal government could be implemented. The bill required close cooperation between the water management district and Department of Environmental Protection and, in a momentary change of heart for the state legislature, authorized the Board of Trustees of the Internal Improvement Trust Fund to

> "...acquire by the exercise of the power of eminent domain any land or water areas and related resources and property, and any and all rights, title, and interest in such land or water lying within the boundaries of the Big Cypress Area and Big Cypress Natural Preserve Addition. The legislature finds that the exercise of the power of eminent domain within the Big Cypress Area and Big Cypress National Preserve Addition to accomplish the purposes of this section is necessary and for a public purpose." [126]

Tallahassee was careful to reiterate Indian rights stating that "...members of the Miccosukee Tribe of Indians of Florida and members of the Seminole Tribe of Florida may continue their usual and customary use and occupancy of lands and waters within the Big Cypress Area, including hunting, fishing, and trapping on a subsistence basis and traditional tribal ceremonies."[127] The "ceremonies" referred mainly to the Green Corn Dance, a private ritual that required some land be cleared and chickees built. It was a celebration generally held in the early summer. The sites and number of dances held varied each year but formed an important means of expressing Tribal solidarity and renewal.

But, being Florida, the tale did not end there. What President Reagan was referring to as the "exchange proposal" would reach all the way to Arizona. It would modify how the Addition Lands and part of the Panther Preserve were paid for and ultimately affect another Tribe over 2,000 miles to the west.

INDIAN SCHOOL

The Indian Industrial Boarding School was founded in Phoenix, Arizona in 1891 to prepare Native American children for assimilation into the hegemonous culture. The idea was that interaction with White people on a daily basis was an important aspect of cultural integration. Operating much like a military school it was racially segregated until it eventually changed its curriculum to recognize cultural pluralism in the 1950s.

As the Phoenix metropolitan area grew the school land became more valuable. After Barron Collier's death in 1976, the family holdings were split and one of the entities, retaining the name of the original company although based in Florida, decided to expand operations to Arizona. In many ways the Indian School had already served whatever purposes it was designed for; the property was ripe for development. The city of Phoenix controlled zoning of the property and the Inter-Tribal Council of Arizona (ITAC), composed of 21 of the 22 tribes in the state as well as the Navajo nation, had a vested interest because closing the school would impact their educational programs.

ARIZONA-FLORIDA LAND EXCHANGE

Rep. Morris Udall (D-AZ) introduced a bill in April 1988 initially proposing $35 million and 108,000 acres of Florida land in exchange for 68 acres in Phoenix. Finally passed in November, Public Law 100–696, authorized the exchange of 111 acres at the school site for the 108,000 acres of sensitive land in south Florida with no cash payment. The school would be closed in 1990. The bill set a minimum value of $80 million on the property but required a reappraisal once the City of Phoenix decided on rezoning. It would sunset in November 1991 if a final valuation and full exchange agreement could not be reached.

While the bill authorized the Collier companies to negotiate with the city it really wasn't for 111 acres. There was a set aside of 16 acres for a Department of Veterans Affairs hospital and care facility, and another 20 acres for a city park, leaving only about 75 acres for development.

Another part of the package, one that would later become a point of contention, was $34.9 million that the Collier companies would pay to a trust fund set up for the education of Native Americans. It was a balloon note with interest payments of approximately $2.9 million due each year and the principal balance in 2026.

The project attracted attention. The initial $80 million value was based on the assumption that new zoning would permit up to 4.4 million sq. ft. of commercial space. Phoenix was a growth market and nine separate designs were offered to the City Council. One, from a committee chaired by a former member of the U. S. House of Representatives, recommended 6.5 million sq. ft. be dedicated to commercial development and valued the property at $86 million. The council decided to pitch them all and adopted one in June 1991 with 1.5 million sq. ft. of commercial space, 1,200 residential apartments and an enlarged park.

As with most legislation the U.S. General Accounting Office (GAO) was asked to look at the deal following the zoning set out by the city, but could not assign a specific value because "... the plan does not represent the property's highest and best use as evaluated by a reasonable and prudent person." The city's approved plan had included a 40-acre park and the report stated that it might be "... likely to attract transients and undesirable park visitors." [128]

To break the logjam, in July the Interior Department formally offered the school land to the Collier interests for $80 million. Six days later the offer was rejected with the proviso that the property would be put up for auction and Collier would have the first right of refusal at 5% above the highest bid. Interior then advertised in 20 different newspapers across the country, but at 1.5 million sq. ft. commercial there was no interest. So during the late summer and fall meetings were held by the Phoenix Planning Commission and on October 23 it recommended construction of 1.8 million sq. ft. of commercial space on the property in the hope that it might attract some investor interest.

Bidding was closed on October 30; none were received. The following month, after private conversations, the City Council reduced the zoning to 1.1 million sq. ft. of commercial space and suggested a trade of 57 acres of the Indian School property and another for two blocks in the middle of downtown Phoenix. With that the deal was signed and sealed. The exchange would proceed.

One of the critical elements was that the Florida properties owned by Collier and the payment to the Indian trust be equal in value to the government property in Phoenix. However, a second GAO report to Congress stated that:

> "For several reasons, we cannot conclude that the Florida properties, along with the $34.9 million to be paid by Collier to the Indian Trust Funds, equal value of Collier's portion of the Indian School property. The Florida land, which was possibly overvalued in 1998, has not been revalued since then, and its value could have decreased, like other real estate in the United States." [129]

Three of four tracts of the Collier land had been recently appraised by Interior. The fourth tract was the problematic one because it was adjacent to SR 84 (Everglades Parkway) scheduled to be upgraded to limited access I-75. The government had planned to pay the difference between the value of the fourth tract less what had already been paid by Florida and the Federal Highway Administration. Taking that into account, the tract according to the GAO was:

> "...possibly overvalued primarily because the appraiser attached a premium value to this tract because it would have highway frontage for which Collier had previously received compensation. Thus, while Collier was receiving damages from the highway program for a loss in value because of highway construction, Interior was paying a premium for the remaining property because of the highway." [130]

The former Indian School land would be used as collateral against the promised $34.9 million payable to the trust fund. Documents signed in October 1992 transferred ownership of the property with the proviso that the deal close within the next four years. The downtown property of about 7½ acres was also secured by a lien as collateral to ensure payments to the fund.

Approximately 20,000 of the 108,000 acres transmitted was dedicated to creation of the Ten Thousand Islands National Wildlife Refuge to be managed by the U. S. Fish and Wildlife Service with the most important piece the narrow 15,000 acre strip running down the east side of SR 29 from Sunniland to Everglades City. For the balance of the acreage, a little more than 83,000 would be added to the Big Cypress Preserve with the remaining acres to the Panther Refuge.

THE REFUGE

To sum it all up, in 1989, with the Addition Lands legislation pending and an anticipated land transfer from the Indian School exchange and encouraged by local citizens and state organizations such as Florida Wildlife Federation, the USFWS purchased 24,300 acres of hunting and cattle grazing land from the Collier family. Located in the heart of panther territory and bordering on the Fakahatchee, Picayune Strand and Big Cypress, the Refuge would serve as a major connector between large swaths of public land that had been put into public ownership in the 1970s and 1980s. The price was $10.3 million paid for under the authority of the Endangered Species Act.

The Arizona–Florida Land Exchange Act of 1988, after being signed in 1992, added another 4,000 acres to the Panther Refuge. Superficially, it appeared as a pittance given the vast acreage in the Addition Lands given to the Big Cypress, but in reality it was Ford and the Florida panther that got the whole process started.

While the Refuge was bordered on the west above I-75 by SR 29, it gave the water management district another opportunity to restore sheet flow over the 25 sq. mi. acquired. It had little effect on the Refuge, but increased potential rehydration south in the Fakahatchee and southwest in the Picayune Strand. But despite all the good things that came from the Addition Lands purchase and the Indian School exchange, the story had an unhappy ending.

COLLIER DEFAULTS

After establishing a trust fund for the education of Native Americans who were losing their high school, interest payments were made each year until 2012 when the Barron Collier Company defaulted on payments and property taxes.

Upon default it was determined that the company owed over $50 million to the government. The case ended up in court, and ITCA members were told to reduce the scope of educational programs and place any construction of new facilities on hold.

The case wound its way through the courts until July 2017 when a settlement agreement was reached. The company agreed to pay $16 million in back interest but would be released from any further obligation to pay either future interest through the year 2026 or the $34.9 million of principal. The company agreed to turn over a 15 acre plot on the school site to the government, but the 7½ acres in downtown Phoenix was not included because the Interior Department had released collateral liens on the property in 1998 and 2007 before default.

This created a significant shortfall for the Arizona Tribes. Terry Rambler, Chair of the San Carlos Apache Tribe was appalled.

"In Arizona, Tribes have been struggling for decades to find sufficient funding to bring our children home from boarding schools and provide a quality education for them on our tribal lands. The educational trust funds created by Congress upon the closure of the Phoenix Indian School were supposed to provide a sustained source of funding to help this process. Now we are left waiting and hoping that the United States will follow through on its commitment to Indian education in Arizona, which we view as the specific intent of Congress under the act. When the United States makes a promise under the law it should keep it." [131]

From the dry desert of Arizona, we return to the coast of southwest Florida, and the story of a once pristine river, clear, clean and free flowing. It had been altered by the Tamiami Trail and its restoration became the focus of one man's effort and attention for decades.

Turner River

Franklin Adams waxed lyrical as he reflected back on one of Southwest Florida's free flowing streams, and as he became a driving force for restoration described in his thoughts throughout this chapter.

> *The Turner River, it was a beautiful river; it was a perfect setting. And I remember you could see clear to the bottom, down some six feet right near the mouth. When we camped along the Turner it was usually on the slightly higher elevation of a shell midden. The water was clear and when we would bathe to cool off you could pick up old clam or oyster shells from the bottom and all kinds of benthic critters would go skittering all over the place.*
>
> *It was a productive nursery area, but can no longer function as it is now just filled with detritus and sediment due to the cleansing flowage which once occurred. The*

two headwater lakes up north of the Tamiami Trail are eutrophic, so down river it begins to destroy sea grasses and almost everything else. The answer to the problem was to put in a few more culverts. They tried to go in on the south but it was really dense and the road depleted. They couldn't get very far in so that did not work. But you need to do a lot more than that. There are a number of shell mounds down there on almost every river but this one has some really good ones. When I tried to do something about the Turner I worked on it for a long time but obviously it was not enough.

The historic Turner had its headwaters in the mixed hammocks and marshlands of the Big Cypress National Preserve. Nine miles long it meandered through a series of hardwoods and prairies emptying eventually into the Chokoloskee Estuary of Everglades National Park. It was one of the few true freshwater rivers in Southwest Florida.

The old Turner River Gulf Station was just west of Ingram Billie's village on the south side of the Trail also. After a canoeing trip we would often walk down to the Gulf station to get cold Pepsis. An elderly lady named Ms. Holzman ran the station. Her husband was an invalid and we enjoyed listening to this nice lady as she told us stories about the building of the Tamiami Trail and showed us an album of old photos. There is a great amount of history on and around the Turner.

To the northeast was Ingram Billie's corn dance village on a hidden hammock in the Turner River Swamp. My brother John attended the corn dance there and was told by an Indian friend that this location was a hideout and garden for the Indians during the Seminole wars. In the center of the river were tall tripod appearing structures made from cypress opposite the Indian village. Not certain what they were used for, perhaps drying hides in the past. Years later a man named Rogers purchased the woods on the north side of the Tamiami Trail and put in the "Turner River Jungle Gardens" for tourists. He decided to begin airboat rides down the Turner and so he removed all the old tripod structures from the river. In addition the old cabbage palm that grew across the narrow part of the river which blocked going down stream in the spring was cut out.

SR 839

In the 1960s infrastructure in Florida was designed and built for one purpose: to support development. With an east-west toll road called the Everglades Parkway bisecting Collier County on the north, and the Tamiami Trail on the south, two north-south dirt roads were built from borrow material dredged up to create canals and dry out adjacent

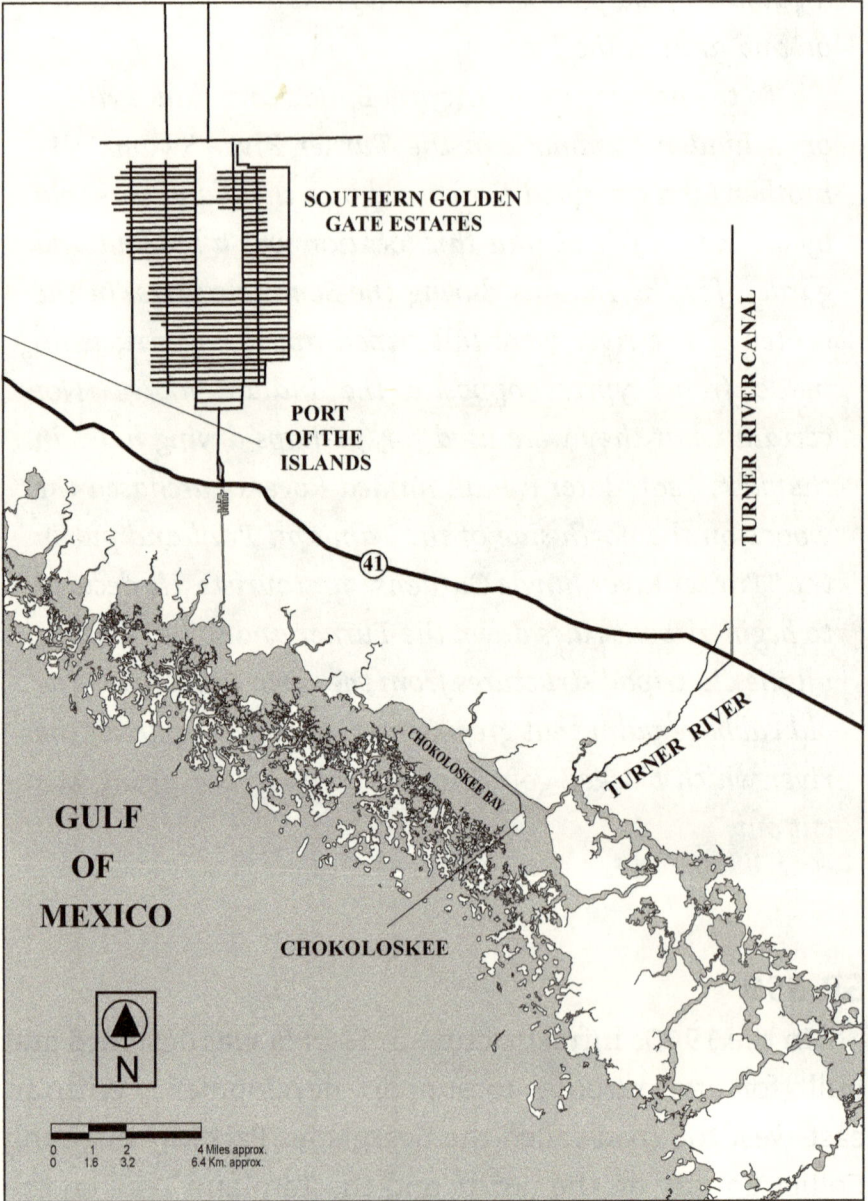

Turner River.
Map created by John G. Beriault.

land: the Turner River road SR 839 and canal and the Birdon road SR 841 and canal. A small connector called the Wagon Wheel road was built to SR 29.

The Turner River canal was 35 feet wide and served as the major conveyance tied into the Alligator Alley canal down past the Tamiami Trail. It cut off the upper reaches of the river and severed surface flow which had helped raise the level.

Why that road was built and for what reason is a total mystery except that the Colliers owned the land and it looked as though there was some road money available to Collier County. They had a desire to build the road and to construct it they had to go several miles up into the Turner River swamp. They dug this canal like they always do in South Florida—to get the fill or the borrow for the roadbed, and what this did was to cut off the natural flow into the headwaters lake that formed the Turner River.

The overall grand plan was for commercial centers and homes to be built along the roads, but it never took place.

The problem went on to south of the Trail and short circuited that part of the river—in fact isolated it. So this caused saltwater intrusion and reduction of the hydroperiods and the residence time water was flowing across the land. The old river began to silt up and get closed up with weeds. It became almost unnavigable.

With the jetport controversy settled, and the Big Cypress dedicated as a National Preserve in 1974, the ground had shifted dramatically. The conservation community was organized as never before, and the long-term effects of projects were being scrutinized with a different lens.

Guidance set forth in the Organic Act of 1916, establishing the National Park Service, set forth its mission: "...to conserve the scenery and the natural and historic objects and the wildlife therein and to provide for the enjoyment of the same in such manner and by such means as will leave them unimpaired for the enjoyment of future generations." [132] The Turner River qualified in all aspects.

"HISTORIC OBJECTS"

As to "historic objects" the Turner had been investigated by archaeologists beginning in 1918. An excavation by William Sears, from the University of Florida, produced a number of artifacts from 30 mounds in a large settlement. The mounds, primarily of oyster shells, had been started on mud flats along the eastern bank and Sears hypothesized the dwellers purposely moved the village towards the water as they built out the mounds. Potsherds excavated were from about 200 BCE to 900 CE with the later dates likely from Calusa occupation at the southern reaches of the Tribe's empire. With the evidence in hand, the Turner River site was named to the National Register of Historic Places in 1970.

> *Those days we couldn't afford a motorboat so we would row up the river past the mounds and snook were just all over the place so there were never questions as to what would be for supper or anything like that.*

"ENJOYMENT OF THE SAME"

Prior to dredging the SR 839 canal, rivers in southwest Florida were a major attraction for fishermen and tourists. The *Star of the Everglades* was one of the first touring boats, built by Gregorio Lopez who came to Florida in 1873 and settled along a small stream southeast of Chokoloskee later called the Lopez River. An avid plume hunter he moved into the tourist industry when the decimated bird population was protected by federal and state law, taking fishermen from Everglade down as far as the Shark River for snook, redfish and tarpon. When the Rod and Gun Club of Everglades City opened, he purchased another vessel, 40 feet long, to take out larger parties. By 1940 Lopez's granddaughter took over the business with the last version of the *Star,* a 65 footer built with bed- rooms, bathrooms, galley and dining area to cruise the entire lower Ten

Thousand Islands, exploring many remote bays, one of which was the mouth of the Turner River.

WISH LIST

The Friends of the Everglades in one of our meetings put together a wish list for Everglades' repair that was published in the newsletter. This list eventually became part of the foundation for Gov. Graham's "Save our Everglades" program. At that time I was the Collier County chairman of Friends of the Everglades so I told Art Marshall that we should put the Turner River on our list. He and Marjory Douglas agreed. I had canoed, explored and camped on this Big Cypress River since I was in high school. This wild little river had been damaged by the building of a road to nowhere which is today known as the Turner River Road. I wanted the National Park Service to plan its repair. Well, Pete Rosendahl had been a student of Art's and he worked for Everglades National Park, so with Art's help we were able to get Pete and David Sikkema to do a mapping study with recommendations to repair the Turner River.

In December 1976, Adams wrote John Good, Superintendent of Everglades National Park, about the use of motorized vehicles in the Park and Big Cypress. While ostensibly dealing with the issue of off-road vehicles, the letter went on to suggest that access to the Turner River be limited at the Tamiami Trail bridge to non-motorized vessels such as canoes and kayaks.

Back in the early '60s and over the years I became a disciple of Art Marshall (the late Arthur Marshall) and I began to learn how systems work and how important it is to keep the systems together. So I began reading about restoration that had been taking place throughout other areas of the country and listen to Art talk about restoring the Everglades and the Big Cypress.

Adams decided his beloved river was his top priority and in July 1978 again wrote John Good stating that at a workshop on the Big Cypress he learned the Department of the Interior was seriously considering restoration. Good responded that he, accompanied by an archaeologist, had canoed the river down to the estuary. By 1981 the Park Service had produced a management plan for the river and made it available for public comment.

Pete Rosendahl of the NPS had put together a plan for restoration with the help of Friends of the Everglades and with Rosendahl helping we all put our heads together. Pete was a hydrologic engineer and we had a good plan for restoring the river, the M-621 plan. The river was still there; it just had to be put back together.

The plan called for 19 new plugs and 8 culverts. Submitted to the South Florida Water Management District, the matter of who would pay arose immediately. Art Marshall was on it. Interior didn't have it in the budget, so Marshall proposed that Collier County pay. The Water Management Board (WMB) at the county approved the plan and sent it to the commission without a suggestion as to where the money might come from.

On a parallel track, the Corps had reviewed and submitted for comment a Clean Water Act Sec. 404 permit for the plan. With that, the nest was poked and the hornets came flying out. The main concern was that rehydrating the watershed would negatively impact inholdings grandfathered in the Big Cypress. An internal memo between the two affected Interior superintendents recounted the advice of the Solicitor General affirming that the federal government would be liable for damages to property but that it would be "... almost impossible to determine if high water levels, which naturally occur, were in fact caused by any government restoration or were simply part of the natural cycle as they were this year." [133] With that they pushed ahead and in June 1983 the district approved installation of new culverts and plugs.

At that point, the process stalled. Property owners rallied their forces and WMB staff was ordered to assess the impact on each parcel–an impossible task given the subtle changes in elevation that were hard to measure even with laser scanning technology. Most of the parcels were adjacent to roadways: the Turner River road, Tamiami Trail and Everglades Parkway, the two-lane toll road to the north. Lots had been purchased for commercial development meaning lawyers would be involved and owners would not give in easily.

Adams, in an attempt to keep the project moving forward, wrote Fred Fagergren, Superintendent of the BCNP in September 1985.

"After our meeting I discussed the Turner River project with the Environmental Coalition at our monthly meeting also talked with Benedict, and Profitt, and others. I understand that you have met with some of them subsequently. Please call me if you need any help at any time. I will give you a call regarding the Colliers. Have mentioned Turner River to them briefly, but could meet with Cliff Barksdale, their engineer, if you have not already done so." [134]

> *There was a lot of discussion at the time. There were some small landholders objecting, but you've always got to deal with the Colliers. They owned the land, most of the land.*

With a push from Adams and others to keep pressure on the reluctant county, Gov. Graham was blunt in a 1986 letter to Commissioner John Pistor:

> "I request your assistance and support for a project critical to the restoration of the hydrology of the Big Cypress National Preserve. I request that Collier County quitclaim the lands necessary for the restoration of the Turner River. Restoration cannot occur unless ownership of these canals rests with the U. S. Government." [135]

Despite pressure from the governor, the county attorney in a report to the commission opined that "... (it) has been determined that Collier County could be held at least partially liable for any property damage suits caused by the new management plan for the canal." [136] The federal government would not indemnify the county, but asserted that if any litigation occurred the Interior Department would be held liable because "... restoration of the Everglades is mandated by the United States Legislature." [137]

Yet the county, despite assurances from Washington and Tallahassee, still refused to quit claim the road and the canal bottom. Preferring to spend another year evaluating the impact of abandoning the Turner River canal, the commission voted to approve another study 5- 0.

RESTORATION BEGINS

In 1988 federal funds became available to implement the 1981 plan, taking the county off the financial and legal hook. Buyouts of private owners began to pick up, and a number of plugs and upstream culverts were installed. Further south, near the headwaters area two culverts were added to increase flow into the waterway and plugs were added to stop drainage from leaking into the SR 29 canal.

The County quitclaimed deed to the road and canal to the National Park Service so it could go ahead with restoration of the Turner River road, Wagon Wheel road and Birdon that adjoins it. The Park Service had begun putting into culverts, putting in cement blocks, dams and weirs to divert the water back into the two headwater lakes north of the river, to reestablish the old historical flow and eventually reduce the depth of that ditch south of the trail. They are trying to put the system back together and when they do it will be the first restoration of a river in Florida.

The method used to clear both sediment and weeds from the river never worked. A later attempt to remove vegetation mechanically temporarily cleared the channel but the weeds quickly grew back. The main problem was that despite the plugs and culverts there wasn't sufficient pressure to clear the sediment. A second problem was that some fish species, attempting to escape encroaching salinity pushing upstream during dry season, ending up at the lowest plug blocking their path and soon perished.

A better solution became available in 1996 when wetland mitigation money was used to fill in the downstream part of the Turner River canal. While some of the rock and spoil had been used for roadbed there were piles left on both sides of the canal which could easily be pushed into direct flow back to the original channel. This also had a dynamic effect upon vegetation growth in the river as flow was increased substantially.

Minor changes have been made to the river over the past decade, but it will simply never be what it once was for Franklin Adams.

Collier Seminole State Park

COLLIER FAMILY GIFT

In the southwestern corner of Collier County was Royal Palm Hammock, the site of a stand of native royal palm trees, one of only three in Florida. It was first owned by the Southern States Land and Timber Company which reserved 150 acres to be made into a national park. The company had been established in 1877 by Jules Burguières, active in experiments for growing sugar in South Florida.

When Barron Gift Collier bought the County ten years later he approached the National Park Service, offering to donate coastal land to be named Lincoln-Lee National Park. He was rebuffed because it was a tiny piece of land with little historical significance. In response Collier then added another 6,273 acres in 1924 and again offered the land to the federal government, but the offer was once again rejected.

The problem lay less with Collier's offer than with bureaucratic bungling. When his idea floated up to Washington, the Park Service had its hands full in trying to establish its place in the pantheon of existing government agencies. The "Organic Act" creating the National Park Service had been signed into law by Pres. Woodrow Wilson in August 1916.[138] As a new federal agency the Park Service soon faced withering attacks from the National Forest Service which was more interested in timbering than preserving. Livestock growers complained about the possibility of grazing rights being taken away by the new federal agency and a contingent of politically powerful individuals from Arizona and California wanted to dam the Colorado River.

SEMINOLE CONNECTION

When Collier died in 1939 his family continued to press for the National Park designation. Graham Copeland, originally hired to build the Tamiami Trail, was an engineer and surveyor who took up the cause. As he built the road, he located a number of abandoned forts used during the Seminole Wars as well as some former Indian villages. He later became a Collier County Commissioner and was so fascinated with the history of south Florida that he created a series of plaques mounted on concrete pedestals to memorialize the sites. This led him to research the history of the Seminole Wars in Florida, and to design a block house similar to structures from some of the old forts way back in the 1840s and 1850s. He located it in the park where it stands today having survived the elements for over 80 years. Because of the lack of records it is difficult to know how the Seminole name became appended to the Collier name, but was most likely through the historical

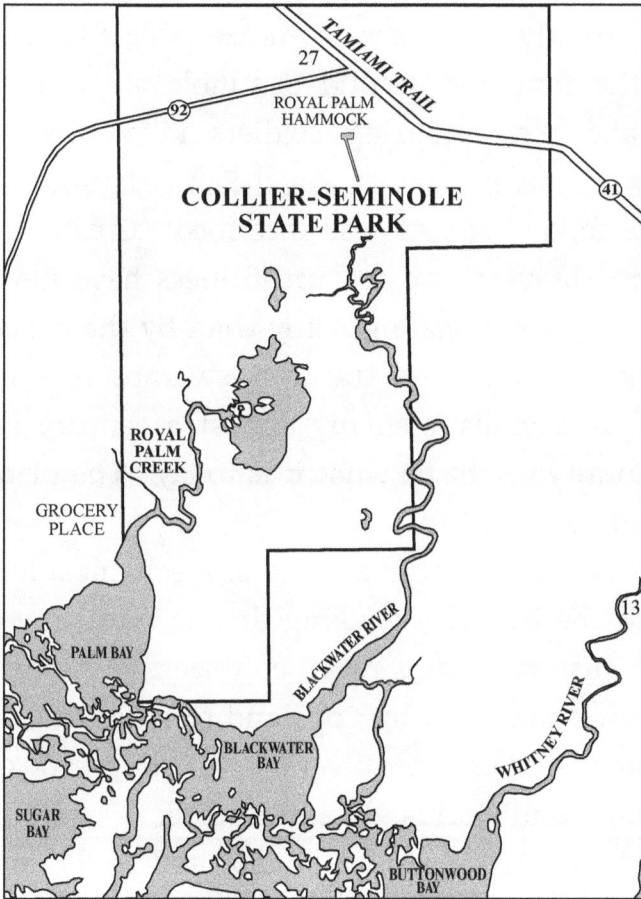

Collier-Seminole State Park.
Map created by John G. Beriault.

research and work of Copeland, with the support of the Collier family.

Many of the records on establishment of the park were destroyed by hurricane Donna in 1960 when the courthouse in Everglades City was flooded. What is known is that a neoclassical monument to Barron Collier was dedicated on January 1, 1941, and maps after that listed Barron Collier Memorial Park in its present location. There were apparently a number of bronze tablets about battles during the first and second Seminole wars chronicling battles and memorializing soldiers killed and naming Indian warriors. In one, at Royal Palm Hammock in the park, the following text was inscribed: "Greater courage, intrepidity, bravery and resourcefulness have never been possessed by any invading Army than by the officers and men who explore these trackless swamps in pursuit of a valiant and vigilant enemy almost a century ago that Collier County might be what it is today." The plaque was also dated January, 1941.

In 1944 the American Society of Mechanical Engineers dedicated the Bay City walking dredge number 849 as a national historic mechanical engineering landmark. It was the machine used by Copeland to build the Tamiami Trail from the Blackwater River to the Belle Meade crossing where US 41 and Florida 951 intersected.

The dredge had a 50 hp engine and could "walk" 60 feet in 45 seconds using retractable feet at the four corners of the machine and two large pods at the center of the apparatus to lift it up and move it until the four corner feet could be lowered to stabilize the entire platform. The 30' wide dredge had a large single bucket to scrape up the muck and place it alongside the borrow canal to form an elevated roadbed. When the muck gave way to limestone rock, dynamite was used to blow the rock apart and the dredge would move, pick it up, and place it on what would become roadbed base. The machine was capable of creeping across the landscape at the rate of about 1 mile per day in muck, but much less when there was rock that had to be dynamited.

The efforts of Copeland and the family failed to make an impression on the National Park Service so they finally gave up and deeded the land over to Collier County, and in March 1944 the county turned ownership over to the Florida Park Service. The Service was the outgrowth of a number of attempts to preserve Civil War battlefields that the state had purchased as historic sites. With a number of memorials, but little management, the legislature had introduced a bill in 1925 to create the Florida State Park system, but provided no money. Two years later the legislature created the State Board of Forestry and in 1935 the Florida Park Service. Then, in 1941 the legislature merged forestry and parks putting the Park Service under the state forester, a somewhat uncomfortable position until after the Second World War when the state finally acknowledged the differences between forestry and park management and separated the two.

After World War II the state partially developed the site with a campground and dedicated it as Collier–Seminole State Park in 1947. The main natural attraction was a stand of royal palms, the tall and stately trees at the edge of a rare rockland hammock at the extreme northern end of its range.[139] The block house built probably by Copeland, the neoclassical memorial and a small campground were all available to visitors. Dedication of the land as a state park was never the first choice of the Collier family. If it could not be designated as an independent federal park, they wanted it connected it to the larger Everglades National Park also dedicated in 1947. It would have been the ideal entry to the larger park, but didn't make the cut.

In 1969 the State of Florida connected the headwaters of the Blackwater River to a canal and boat ramp for a canoe and kayak launch site. Today, it has 7,200 acres and is home to a number of listed species and available for camping as well as boating. Over 6,400 acres remains as raw land with mangroves, cypress and pine forested uplands, much as it was when the Calusa roamed the coast.

Putting It All Together

LANDSCAPE MODIFICATION

The Glades culture and later Calusa used south Florida as a resource not for exploitation, but for survival. Inland areas, while less habitable, provided deer and smaller animals while the coast provided an abundance of fish and shellfish. Settlements located where there was potable water. People regarded the environment as central to their very existence, modified it when necessary, and took from it only what they needed for nutrition and for personal decoration.

Early White settlers and the disenfranchised began to move in before and during the Civil War. They avoided the swamps and marshes of the Everglades, preferring to live along the coast. While battered by the rains of summer and autumn, coupled with occasional devastating hurricanes, they accepted the fact that the ravages of nature could only be coped with and endured, but not overcome.

In the late 1800s, an appreciation of the natural value of Florida's fertile soil and productive estuaries brought small farmers and fisherman. Visitors began to come too, but few ventured past the end of the railroad line or the steamship dock.

In the early part of the 20th century fishing and agriculture were the main occupations of settlers along the southwest coast. Farming in the Big Cypress and along the riverbanks was hard, but the Seminoles and Miccosukee knew where soil with adequate nutrients existed, and how to minimize saltwater intrusion into their fields, and what to grow and where. Those lessons were passed along during an era of cooperation following the Seminole Wars as a few hardy souls opened stores and traded with the natives. Later came small semi-industrial operations to harvest mangroves for tannin and a thriving clam processing industry at Marco Island, but small-scale fishing and farming dominated for years.

As farming became more mechanized the scale of operations increased, requiring irrigation systems to deliver water to farms and fertilizers as needed. But then, with rail and road access expanding, and as air conditioning and mosquito control came into play, commercial and residential development of the land began.[140]

Manmade canals dried out wetlands like the Picayune Strand, logging trams crisscrossed the Fakahatchee. Obedient to the old saw that "dry land is good and wet land is useless," roads like SR 29 and canals like the Golden Gate and the Cocohatchee were built to move water from inland to the coast. But they did more than that. They acted as entry points for exotic fish and plant life to enter the ecosystem and, as the surface of the land dried out, invited salt intrusion into the lower level aquifers where many communities drew their water, and in the process altered the chemistry of habitat formed over hundreds of years disrupting native species unable to cope with the abrupt change.

The establishment of small inland communities like Pinecrest and Poinciana had little impact at the time. The Tamiami Trail was a different matter. It disrupted land and water flow in a part of the state that few people occupied permanently but where many began to visit. Marjory Douglas' southern region was made into a national park in 1947; that same year the C&SF project was authorized. It would mainly affect the rapidly growing east coast of Florida. Roads and canals were being built and regarded as uniformly beneficial until the L-28 canal began to affect Everglades Park's water and the Big Cypress jetport became more than the Miami Dade Port Authority's dream. That began a seminal period, the five years between 1965 and 1970, when state-wide environmental groups coalesced and organized into an influential whole as the Everglades Coalition while on the west coast the Conservancy and others were concentrating their resources on acquiring coastal assets in Rookery Bay and the Ten Thousand

Islands. Together they began to slowly change the way Floridians viewed their abundant natural resources.

RESTORATION

Changing the mindset of development at any cost involved a number of factors. To begin with, much of the land acquired for public benefit and use was owned by first and second generation family members. They lived and worked in south Florida and were committed to good stewardship. Decisions could be made quickly until the third and fourth generations began to spread ownership throughout the country adding pressure to monetize hard assets. The Collier family companies, with Collier-Seminole State Park, the Fakahatchee, Panther Preserve and Rookery Bay, established a tradition of benign paternalism as did Ben Hill Griffin, Sr. with his willingness to help save the threatened Corkscrew watershed.[141]

In addition to the founding families, much of the public land described in this book was saved because a group of committed men and women, supported by politicians willing to buck the special interests, realized that something had been lost that needed to be brought back and returned to as near its original state as possible. They believed they could help mend what had been broken and place it in a state of permanent equilibrium insofar as possible, but to do so needed a clear path and equitable compensation for landowners.

I must mention that much of what we have accomplished in moving towards the goal of restoring south Florida has been built upon the foundation laid by grassroots individuals who labored long and fought for many years. Many of the battles had to be fought more than once. Many of the old warriors have worn out or passed on to their reward. New and younger volunteers are now involved and that's encouraging. In fact it's absolutely vital.

Third, a succession of governors understood the need for a balanced approach to development and created an integrated process of planning coordinated at the state, regional and local levels. The key element was a sense of bipartisanship as the governor's office was occupied during the 40 years from 1967 to 2007 by an equal number of Republicans and Democrats beginning with Claude Kirk and ending with Jeb Bush.

The legislature, with support of citizen initiatives, provided the means to buy land for public use and benefit with the Florida Environmental Land and Water Management Act, Land Conservation Act and Environmentally Endangered Lands Act all passed in 1972, the Conservation and Recreation Lands Act of 1979, Save Our Rivers Act in 1981 and later Preservation 2000 passed in 1989, continued as Florida Forever a decade later.

Today, we still need ongoing resources to not only restore but also to manage what we, as citizens, now own. One view is that we should abandon the concept of growth and development and favor restorative economics. But to parse the words carefully "growth" means an increase in physical dimensions, and "development" means an improvement in the quality of goods and services and resources that we use. In south Florida the two seem inseparable, but need not be. A restorative economy affirms that the number or size of possessions we own or use is less important than our quality of life. The key factor is sustainability whereby the production of goods and services available to people is being met without a reduction in the capacity of the environment to provide those goods and services necessary for the future. The goal is: "Leave the world better than you found it, take no more than you need, try not to harm life or the environment, make amends if you do." [142] In the broadest sense, exploitation of southwest Florida for short term gains created long term problems, some unforeseen and others quite apparent.

Obviously, we will never restore the Big Cypress or Fakahatchee or Picayune Strand or Turner River to what they were before being logged, dug up, paved over and intersected by roads and canals, but we can look to the future where nearly 200,000 acres of partially developed land in eastern Collier County and another 80,000 acres in the Lee County DRGR that replenishes the aquifers for populous Fort Myers are once again being keyed for development. The sheer scale requires that the land be managed for the next 50 years in a way that benefits the health of the overall and not the few.

It will not be easy. There are exogenous factors that bear upon the future. The examples of the 11-mile road story and seismic activities in the Big Cypress all depend upon the world price of oil. At a certain level, it is no longer profitable, but that is beyond our control.

There is also the feeling among some county commissioners and staff that with over 70% of Collier County in public lands that is enough. And the Lee County commission has quietly decided that building homes and commercial centers in the aquifer recharge area will be fine. At an even higher level, the SFWMD has over 452,000 acres that it either owns or has in conservation easements—344,000 acres are available for public use.[143] Some say that's plenty. It's much the same argument that John Jones ran into in Tallahassee when trying to get the state to buy the Big Cypress. The resistance then was "we already have enough wet land; we don't need any more." [144]

Private property rights have to be respected but the debate should not be framed at the extremes as a battle between capitalism and socialism, or bandied about as coastal elites setting their wishes against the common person. To eschew this requires a degree of political maturity, a rare commodity in our country today.

We need to create a process whereby the pumping out of aquifers, polluting of our rivers and estuaries, destruction of the fertility of the soil and replacing it with fertilizers, depleting coastal resources and fragmenting wildlife habitat is viewed as destructive. It's not that these resources are irreplaceable or that they cannot be modified or put back together in some semblance of their original condition. But one ounce of prevention is worth one pound of mitigation, and as a society we sometimes depend too much on engineered solutions, to be applied sometime in the future, to solve our immediate problems once they appear.

There are instances where mitigation works within the immediate vicinity of the disturbed area of flora or fauna. There are parts of the landscape, such as the Sending Lands of the Collier County Rural Fringe, where mitigation banking is encouraged but, in many cases, is far from the location of the disturbance. Finally, mitigation should be a last resort only after preservation and modification have been ruled out. Franklin Adams agrees but is realistic about the future.

We continually hear about Everglades restoration which sounds positive. However, with over fifty percent of the historical Everglades already lost-gone, actual restoration is no longer possible. As Florida's great ecologist and mentor Arthur Marshall said, "We cannot restore the Everglades, but we can repair the remaining Everglades and make them more functional again." We must address the causes of continuing wetland and water quality loss and stop treating the symptoms.

We are rushing toward a future that can be managed if we have a willingness to learn from the lessons of the past, taking from them what worked and what didn't, and using them as a starting point for how to embrace the issues inherent in principles of good growth management and an appreciation of the value of our natural resources.

Franklin has the final words:

Being a native Floridian, now in my 85th year I have truly seen and experienced the tragic and avoidable loss of many important ecological and historical treasures, especially in the Big Cypress and greater Everglades region. There are times when I cannot avoid being angry and frustrated with the continuing greed and indifference by most politicians and their behind-the-scenes funders. Especially, when they continue to ignore the will of the majority of voters who support environmental protection and restoration. But, what alternative do we have left to us? Giving up the fight? No, each of us who care must continue our collective efforts and work to bring others into what we used to call Marjory's Army.

ENDNOTES

1 Dasmann, Raymond. *No Further Retreat: The Fight to Save Florida*. p. 221.

2 Widmer, Randolph. *The Evolution of the Calusa: A Non-agricultural Chiefdom on the Southwest Florida Coast*, p. 176.

3 https://en.wikipedia.org/wiki/Little_Salt_Spring

4 Griffin, John W. *Time and Space in South Florida*. Florida Anthropologist, Sept. 1989, p. 191.

5 Sears, William. The Turner River, Collier County, Florida. Florida Anthropologist, June, 1956 p. 47-60.

6 The Turner would be choked in the 1920s by a road linking Florida's two coasts, but later partially restored through the efforts of conservationists.

7 The author has visited and analyzed this site.

8 8 CR 55 is a listed historic site designated by the University of Florida.

9 https://www.nps.gov/casa/learn/historyculture/native-americans.html.

10 https://www.floridamuseum.ufl.edu/science/investigating-the-calusa.

11 Tebeau, Charlton. *Man in the Everglades: 2000 Years of Human History in the Everglades National Park*, p. 50.

12 https://edis.ifas.edu/pdffiles/AE/AE37500.pdf.

13 https://en.wikipedia.org/wiki/Swamp Land Act of 1850.

14 Tebeau, Charlton. *Florida's Last Frontier: The History of Collier County*, p. 54.

15 Much of this information comes from R. H. Pratt founder of the Carlisle Indian School who went to South Florida to report on the Seminoles in 1879. He gave a fairly full picture of the situation he found which was one of small nucleated farms and cattle ranches. He felt that the communities were prosperous and in those larger villages that he visited successfully organized into camps.

[16] Duever, Michael, John E. Carlson, John F. Meeder, Linda C. Duever, Lance H. Gunderson, Lawrence A. Riopelle, Taylor B. Alexander, Ronald L. Myers and Daniel F. Spangler. *The Big Cypress Reserve*, p. 141.

[17] Tebeau, Charlton. Ibid, p. 101.

[18] Tebeau, Charlton. *Ibid*, p. 116.

[19] Storter, Kirby. *Southeastern Indian Oral History Project*: University of Florida. p. 4.

[20] https://en.wikipedia.org/wiki/Plume hunting.

[21] Derr, Mark. *Some Kind of Paradise: A Chronicle of Man and the Land in Florida.* p. 139.

[22] Davis, Amie. *Recollections of Environmental Changes in the Ten Thousand Islands, Florida Bay and the Everglades: The Oral History and Social Issues of User Groups in Southwest Florida and the Everglades.* p. 29.

[23] Tebeau, Charlton. *Florida's Last Frontier*, p. 224.

[24] Chevelier, started in the 1880s by an alleged plume hunter of the same name, had quite a history. It had purchased the Ed Watson place on Chatham Bend in 1919. After Watson's death (the subject of Peter Mathiessen's book *Killing Mr. Watson*), the company planned to turn the property into a subdivision. It dug a number of canals along the Chatham, but had no overall engineering plan so the water was never properly diverted.

[25] This section is now known as the Loop Road.

[26] Sullivan-Hartung, Maureen. *Hidden History of Everglades City & Points Nearby*, p. 16-17.

[27] Walker, Lorenzo. *Dedication of Tamiami Trail Marker*, digital collections.fiu.edu/Tequesta/files/1959/59_1_103. p. 26.

[28] Tebeau, Charlton. *Florida's Last Frontier*, p. 202.

[29] Duever, Michael, *et al*, p. 266.

[30] *Miami News* February 9, 1929.

[31] Duever, Michael, *et al. Ibid.* p. 375.

[32] Repko, *Ibid*, pp. 13-14.

[33] American Oil and Gas Historical Society: 1943 Sunniland Oil Discovery. See AOGHS.org.

[34] Duever, Michael, *et al, Ibid.* p. 353.

[35] *Miami Herald*, March 3, 2017.

[36] This turned out differently as the last flight of the Concorde landed on a 6,000 foot runway.

37 *Miami News*, July 23, 1957.

38 Mueller, Marti. *Everglades Jetport: Academy Prepares a Model, Science*, October 10, 1969. p. 202–203.

39 *Miami News*, July 17, 1968.

40 Everglades Online.com. *History of the Big Cypress*, p. 3.

41 Derr, Mark, *Ibid.* p. 356.

42 Since the agreement was signed Miami international Airport facilities have undergone modernization to accommodate the growth in traffic.

43 Everglades Online.com. *Ibid*, p. 5.

44 Collier County: *Information Regarding the Area of Critical State Concern Overview of the Areas of Critical State Concern (ACSC)*, p. 2.

45 *Miami Herald*, September 6, 1973.

46 *Ibid*, p.5.

47 From Florida Conservation Coalition notes taken by Jane Heerema, Assistant Editor and Lobbyist May 17, 1974.

48 *Ibid.*

49 *Ibid.*

50 Western Union Mailgram from Franklin Adams to Rep. Guy Spicola, May 20, 1974.

51 Letter from John Jones to Jack Moller, Pembroke Pines, FL, June 21, 2001.

52 *Ibid.*

53 An Act to Establish the Big Cypress National Preserve in the State of Florida, and for other purposes (PL 93 – 440).

54 Heinrich, Rudy. *Fading Footprints: The Frontier Communities in the Big Cypress Swamp*, no page number.

55 Jones, *Ibid.*

56 An Act to Establish the Big Cypress National Preserve in the State of Florida, and for other purposes: Sec. 3(a).

57 Wilderness Act of 1964 (PL 88–577), p. 2.

58 Jones, *Ibid.*

59 An Act to Establish the Big Cypress National Preserve in the State of Florida, and for other purposes: Sec. 5 (a).

[60] Multiple Supreme Court since then decisions have addressed the definition of "waters of the United States." According to the EPA website, in 1985, in *United States v. Riverside Bayview Homes, Inc.*, the U.S. Supreme Court deferred to the Corps' assertion of jurisdiction over wetlands adjacent to a traditional navigable water, stating that adjacent wetlands may be regulated as waters of the United States because they are "inseparably bound up" with navigable waters and "in the majority of cases" have "significant effects on water quality and the aquatic ecosystem" in those waters.

[61] Letter from Robert Brantly to Governor Bob Graham, October 21, 1982.

[62] *Miami Herald,* February 24, 1983

[63] Repko, *Ibid,* p. 35.

[64] Letter from Mel Finn to Jane Parks, October 5, 1964.

[65] Letter from Franklin Adams to Congressman Paul Rogers, 11th District Florida, October 11, 1965.

[66] *Collier County News*, February 11, 1966.

[67] *Ibid,* November 12, 1966.

[68] *Ibid.*

[69] Chapter 67-229, Fla. Stats., was designated as the Florida Uniform Land Sales Practice Law. Section 30, Chapter 478, Fla. Stats., F.S.A., was amended by adding a new Section 478.331, Florida Statutes to allow removal of members.

[70] Nathaniel Reed, Personal papers, undated.

[71] https://www.flsenate.gov/Laws/Statutes/2012/Chapter380/.

[72] *Miami Herald*, Jan 19, 1973.

[73] *Ibid.*

[74] *Miami Herald*, September 12, 1976.

[75] *Fort Myers News-Press*, March 25, 1975.

[76] *Naples Daily News*, June 6, 1976.

[77] Letter from Willard Merrihue to Sen. Lawton Chiles, April 2, 1981.

[78] Collier County: *Information Regarding the Area of Critical State Concern Overview of the Areas of Critical State Concern (ACSC)*, p. 2.

[79] U. S. Army Corps of Engineers. *Comprehensive Everglades Restoration Plan: Picayune Strand Restoration: Final Implementation Report and EIS*, p. iv.

[80] *Ibid,* p. ix.

[81] *Ibid.*

82 South Florida Water Management District: *Just the Facts*, April 2015.

83 https://www.fdacs.gov/ezs3download/download/25619/516499/PSSF%2520FINAL%25202008%2520PLAN

84 Stiff, Bradley *et al. Temperature Inverted Haloclines provide Warm-Water Refugia for Manatees in Southwest Florida. Estuaries and Coasts*, April 2010.

85 Collier County: *Comprehensive Watershed Improvement Plan*, September 23, 2016, p. 38.

86 U. S. Army Corps of Engineers: *Limited Reevaluation Report: Picayune Strand*, undated.

87 Letter from Norman Herren to Joel Kuperberg, September 20, 1967.

88 Letter from Robert Ghiotto, Black, Crow to Joel Kuperberg, March 26, 1968.

89 Audubon had been selected because it was already managing Corkscrew Swamp Sanctuary to the north.

90 *Naples Daily News*, June 12, 1970.

91 The study also measured E. coli for the county health department which forced it to eventually close Henderson Creek to shellfish harvesting.

92 *New York Times*, October 23, 1970.

93 Conservancy of Southwest Florida. *Estuaries Report Card* 2017, p. 144.

94 Dasmann, *Ibid*, p. 70.

95 Joel Kuperberg, personal notes, April 23, 1969.

96 Letter from Joel Kuperberg to Patrick Noonan, vice president, The Nature Conservancy, December 12, 1973.

97 Letter from State Sen. Philip Lewis to Arthur McIntosh February 1, 1977.

98 Waitley, p. 124.

99 Florida Aquatic Preserve Act of 1975 (258.36, F. S.).

100 Whitney, Ellie, p. 179.

101 *Sarasota Sun Sentinel*, August 27, 1989.

102 The LAAC was tasked with providing recommendations for CARL priority list. It was a powerful ally to the CREW effort over the years.

103 Permits issued by the SFWMD and the Corps also had to be approved by the USFWS which had the ability to issue a "jeopardy opinion" if a development had a deleterious effect on wildlife. With multiple agencies involved the process offered environmental organizations time to reflect upon the impact of the permits and file a challenge when necessary.

[104] The National Environmental Policy Act of 1969, (PL 91-190, 42 U.S.C. 4321-4347), January 1, 1970

[105] See *Sylvester vs. the US Army Corps of Engineers*, 884 F.2d. 394. (9th Cir. 1989).

[106] Noted in Congressional Record S 3510, March 31, 1988.

[107] *Miami Herald*, August 11, 1980

[108] *Naples Star*, October 1, 1983.

[109] *Ibid.*

[110] Letter from Joseph Carroll, regional director, to District Engineer U.S. Army Corps of Engineers Jacksonville Florida, July 27, 1983.

[111] Letter from Robert Brantly, executive director, Florida Game and Freshwater Fish Commission to Victoria Tschinkel, executive director, Department of Environmental Regulation, August 15, 1983.

[112] Letter from Charles Lee, vice president, Florida Audubon Society to Richard Rogers, South Florida Water Management District, August 17, 1983.

[113] His brother was editor of the *Washington Post.*

[114] *St. Petersburg Times*, July 16, 1984.

[115] *Fort Myers News-Press*, January 18, 1984.

[116] *Miami Herald*, March 29, 1984.

[117] *Miami Herald*, April 6, 1984.

[118] The commission was rebranded in 1999 as the Florida Fish and Wildlife Conservation Commission.

[119] *Naples Daily News*, April 22, 1984.

[120] *Naples Daily News*, April 19, 1984

[121] *St. Petersburg Times*, July 16, 1984.

[122] *Miami Herald*, May 12, 1984.

[123] Franklin Adams to Jack Lorenz, President Izaak Walton League of America, June 18, 1984.

[124] The Big Cypress National Preserve Addition Act, (S.90, PL 100-301 as amended), Sec. 4 (b) 4.

[125] https://www.presidency.ucsb.edu/documents/statement-signing-the-big-cypress-national-preserve-addition-act.

[126] The Big Cypress Conservation Act of 1973. (FS 380-55 (7)).

127 *Ibid.* FS 380-55 (8).

128 United States General Accounting Office: *Land Exchange: Phoenix Indian School Development Plan as It Affects Property Value,* July, 1991, p. 12.

129 United States General Accounting Office. *Land Exchange: Phoenix and Collier Reach Agreement on Indian School Property*, February, 1992, p. 11.

130 *Ibid,* p. 12.

131 Press Release, Fort Yuma Quechan Tribe, July 19, 2017.

132 An Act to Establish a National Park Service, and Other Purposes, Approved August 25, 1916 (39 Stat. 535), p. 1.

133 Memo from Fred Fagergren, Superintendent Big Cypress National Preserve to Jack Moorhead, Superintendent Everglades National Park, November 12, 1982.

134 Letter from Franklin Adams to Fred Fagergren, September 15, 1985.

135 Letter from Gov. Bob Graham to Commissioner John Pistor, April 4, 1986.

136 Executive Summary: *Discussion on Collier County's Position and Involvement in Maintaining Existing Canals within the Big Cypress National Preserve*, April 28, 1987.

137 *Ibid.*

138 Prior to that there were a number of others including Yellowstone, Sequoia and Yosemite set aside as National Parks in the 1890s. Supported by Pres. Roosevelt, who established five new parks, he also secured passage of the Antiquities Act in 1906 which provided for national monuments and protected antiquities from being taken from public lands.

139 For a full explanation of the rare rockland hammock and its importance, please see https://www.fnai.org/PDFs/NC/Rockland_Hammock_Final_2010.pdf.

140 The Florida Mosquito Control Association was formed in 1922 and the first residential air conditioner was installed in 1914 although it did not become widely available until the 1930s.

141 The Collier companies split into the Barron Collier Company and Collier Enterprises after the death of Barron Collier in 1976.

142 Approximately 30% of Florida is in public land, ranking it 14th among the 50 states. See: Public and Private Land Percentages by U.S. States : Facts & Information : Summit Post.

143 District Lands/ WaterMatters.org (state.fl.us).

144 Hawken, Paul. *The Ecology of Commerce: A Declaration of Sustainability.*

BIBLIOGRAPHY

Carter, Luther J. *The Florida Experience: Land and Water Policy in a Growth State*. Baltimore: Johns Hopkins University Press, 1974.

Dasmann, Raymond. *No Further Retreat: The Fight to Save Florida*. New York: The Macmillan Company, 1971.

Davis, Amie. *Recollections of Environmental Changes in the Ten Thousand Islands, Florida Bay and the Everglades: The Oral History and Social Issues of User Groups in Southwest Florida and the Everglades*. Masters thesis, University of Miami, 1998.

Derr, Mark. *Some Kind of Paradise: A Chronicle of Man and the Land in Florida*. New York: William Morrow Company, 1989.

Duever, Michael, John E. Carlson, John F. Meeder, Linda C. Duever, Lance H. Gunderson, Lawrence A. Riopelle, Taylor B. Alexander, Ronald L. Myers and Daniel F. Spangler. *The Big Cypress Reserve*. New York: National Audubon Society, 1986.

Grunwald, Michael. *The Swamp: The Everglades, Florida, and the Politics of Paradise*. New York: Simon & Schuster, 2006.

Hamilton, Karen. *Lostman's Heritage: Pioneers in the Florida Everglades*. Jupiter: Yesterday Press, 2020.

Heinrich, Rudy. *Fading Footprints: The Frontier Communities in the Big Cypress Swamp*. Middletown, 2021.

Kessler, Martin and Larry Teply. *Jetport: Planning and Politics in the Big Cypress Swamp*. University of Miami Law Review, July 1971.

McCoy, Jack. *Hydrology of Western Collier County Florida*. Tallahassee: U. S. Geological Survey, 1972.

Penniman, Nick. *Nature's Steward: A History of the Conservancy of Southwest Florida*. Sarasota: Pineapple Press, Inc. 2014.

Repko, Marya. *A Brief History of the Fakahatchee*. Everglades City: E City Publishing, 2009.

State of Florida, Department of Agriculture and Consumer Services. *Ten-Year Resource Management Plan for the Picayune Srand State Forest*, Tallahassee. August, 2000.

Sullivan-Hartung, Maureen. *Hidden History of Everglades City & Points Nearby.* Charleston: The History Press, 2010

Tebeau, Charlton. *Florida's Last Frontier: The History of Collier County.* Miami: University of Miami Press, 1957.

Tebeau, Charlton W. *The Story of the Chokoloskee Country.* Miami: University of Miami Press, 1976.

Tebeau, Charlton. *Man in the Everglades: 2000 Years of Human History in the Everglades National Park.* Miami: University of Miami Press, 1976.

Vuic, Jason. *The Swamp Peddlers.* Chapel Hill: The University of North Carolina Press, 2021

Waitley, Douglas. *The Last Paradise: The Building of Marco Island.* Naples: Naples Media Group, 1999.

Whitney, Ellie, D. Bruce Means and Ann Rudloe. *Priceless Florida: Natural Ecosystems and Native Species.* Sarasota, Pineapple Press, 2004.

Widmer, Randolph. *The Evolution of the Calusa: A Non-agricultural Chiefdom on the Southwest Florida Coast.* Tuscaloosa, University of Alabama Press, 1988.

INDEX

www.ingramcontent.com/pod-product-compliance
Lightning Source LLC
Chambersburg PA
CBHW031501270326
41930CB00006B/193